Charities Act 1992

CHAPTER 41

ARRANGEMENT OF SECTIONS

Charities Act 1992 c. **41** iii

Miscellaneous and supplementary

Section
47. Minor and consequential amendments of 1960 Act.
48. Amendment of Charitable Trustees Incorporation Act 1872.
49. Amendment of Redundant Churches and Other Religious Buildings Act 1969.
50. Contributions towards maintenance etc. of almshouses.
51. Fees and other amounts payable to Commissioners.
52. Disclosure of information to and by Commissioners.
53. Data protection.
54. Supply of false or misleading information to Commissioners, etc.
55. Restriction on institution of proceedings for certain offences.
56. Enforcement of requirements by order of Commissioners, and other provisions as to orders made by them.
57. Directions of the Commissioners.

PART II

CONTROL OF FUND-RAISING FOR CHARITABLE INSTITUTIONS

Preliminary

58. Interpretation of Part II.

Control of fund-raising

59. Prohibition on professional fund-raiser etc. raising funds for charitable institution without an agreement in prescribed form.
60. Professional fund-raisers etc. required to indicate institutions benefiting and arrangements for remuneration.
61. Cancellation of payments and agreements made in response to appeals.
62. Right of charitable institution to prevent unauthorised fund-raising.
63. False statements relating to institutions which are not registered charities.

Supplementary

64. Regulations about fund-raising.

PART III

PUBLIC CHARITABLE COLLECTIONS

Preliminary

65. Interpretation of Part III.

Prohibition on conducting unauthorised collections

66. Prohibition on conducting public charitable collections without authorisation.

Permits

67. Applications for permits to conduct public charitable collections.
68. Determination of applications and issue of permits.
69. Refusal of permits.
70. Withdrawal etc. of permits.
71. Appeals.

Charities Act 1992

1992 CHAPTER 41

An Act to amend the Charities Act 1960 and make other provision with respect to charities; to regulate fund-raising activities carried on in connection with charities and other institutions; to make fresh provision with respect to public charitable collections; and for connected purposes.   [16th March 1992]

BE IT ENACTED by the Queen's most Excellent Majesty, by and with the advice and consent of the Lords Spiritual and Temporal, and Commons, in this present Parliament assembled, and by the authority of the same, as follows:—

PART I

CHARITIES

Preliminary

1.—(1) In this Part—

"the 1960 Act" means the Charities Act 1960;

"financial year"—

    (a) in relation to a charity which is a company, shall be construed in accordance with section 223 of the Companies Act 1985; and

    (b) in relation to any other charity, shall be construed in accordance with regulations made by virtue of section 20(2);

"gross income", in relation to a charity, means its gross recorded income from all sources, including special trusts;

"independent examiner", in relation to a charity, means such a person as is mentioned in section 21(3)(a);

"the official custodian" means the official custodian for charities;

"the register" (unless the context otherwise requires) means the register of charities kept under section 4 of the 1960 Act, and "registered" shall be construed accordingly;

Interpretation of Part I, etc.

1960 c.58.

1985 c.6.

"special trust" means property which is held and administered by or on behalf of a charity for any special purposes of the charity, and is so held and administered on separate trusts relating only to that property.

(2) Subject to subsection (3) below, sections 45 and 46 of the 1960 Act (interpretation) shall have effect for the purposes of this Part as they have effect for the purposes of that Act.

(3) A special trust shall not, by itself, constitute a charity for the purposes of sections 19 to 26.

(4) No vesting or transfer of any property in pursuance of any provision of this Part, or of any provision of the 1960 Act as amended by this Part, shall operate as a breach of a covenant or condition against alienation or give rise to a forfeiture.

Registration of charities

The register of charities.

2.—(1) Section 4 of the 1960 Act (the register of charities) shall be amended as follows.

(2) For subsection (1) there shall be substituted—

"(1) The Commissioners shall continue to keep a register of charities, which shall be kept by them in such manner as they think fit."

(3) In subsection (2), after "so excepted" there shall be inserted "(other than one excepted by paragraph (a) of that subsection)".

(4) After subsection (2) there shall be inserted—

"(2A) The register shall contain—

(a) the name of every registered charity; and

(b) such other particulars of, and such other information relating to, every such charity as the Commissioners think fit."

(5) In subsection (4), for paragraph (c) there shall be substituted—

"(c) any charity which has neither—

(i) any permanent endowment, nor

(ii) the use or occupation of any land,

and whose income from all sources does not in aggregate amount to more than £1,000 a year;".

(6) After subsection (7) there shall be inserted—

"(7A) Where any information contained in the register is not in documentary form, subsection (7) above shall be construed as requiring the information to be available for public inspection in legible form at all reasonable times.

(7B) If the Commissioners so determine, that subsection shall not apply to any particular information contained in the register and specified in their determination."

(7) After subsection (8) there shall be inserted—

"(8A) If he thinks it expedient to do so—

(a) in consequence of changes in the value of money, or

(b) with a view to extending the scope of the exception provided for by subsection (4)(c) above,

the Secretary of State may by order amend subsection (4)(c) by substituting a different sum for the sum for the time being specified there.

(8B) Any such order shall be made by statutory instrument subject to annulment in pursuance of a resolution of either House of Parliament.''

(8) Where an exempt charity is on the register immediately before the time when subsection (3) above comes into force, its registration shall cease to have effect at that time.

(9) Section 4 of the 1960 Act, as amended by this section, and with the omission of repealed provisions, is set out in Schedule 1 to this Act.

3.—(1) This section applies to a registered charity if its gross income in its last financial year exceeded £5,000.

(2) Where this section applies to a registered charity, the fact that it is a registered charity shall be stated in English in legible characters—

    (a) in all notices, advertisements and other documents issued by or on behalf of the charity and soliciting money or other property for the benefit of the charity;

    (b) in all bills of exchange, promissory notes, endorsements, cheques and orders for money or goods purporting to be signed on behalf of the charity; and

    (c) in all bills rendered by it and in all its invoices, receipts and letters of credit.

Status of registered charity (other than small charity) to appear on official publications etc.

(3) Subsection (2)(a) has effect whether the solicitation is express or implied, and whether the money or other property is to be given for any consideration or not.

(4) If, in the case of a registered charity to which this section applies, any person issues or authorises the issue of any document falling within paragraph (a) or (c) of subsection (2) in which the fact that the charity is a registered charity is not stated as required by that subsection, he shall be guilty of an offence and liable on summary conviction to a fine not exceeding the third level on the standard scale.

(5) If, in the case of any such registered charity, any person signs any document falling within paragraph (b) of subsection (2) in which the fact that the charity is a registered charity is not stated as required by that subsection, he shall be guilty of an offence and liable on summary conviction to a fine not exceeding the third level on the standard scale.

(6) The Secretary of State may by order amend subsection (1) by substituting a different sum for the sum for the time being specified there.

Charity names

4.—(1) Where this subsection applies to a charity, the Commissioners may give a direction requiring the name of the charity to be changed, within such period as is specified in the direction, to such other name as the charity trustees may determine with the approval of the Commissioners.

Power of Commissioners to require charity's name to be changed.

(2) Subsection (1) applies to a charity if—

    (a) it is a registered charity and its name ("the registered name")—

        (i) is the same as, or

        (ii) is in the opinion of the Commissioners too like,

    the name, at the time when the registered name was entered in the register in respect of the charity, of any other charity (whether registered or not);

    (b) the name of the charity is in the opinion of the Commissioners likely to mislead the public as to the true nature—

        (i) of the purposes of the charity as set out in its trusts, or

        (ii) of the activities which the charity carries on under its trusts in pursuit of those purposes;

    (c) the name of the charity includes any word or expression for the time being specified in regulations made by the Secretary of State and the inclusion in its name of that word or expression is in the opinion of the Commissioners likely to mislead the public in any respect as to the status of the charity;

    (d) the name of the charity is in the opinion of the Commissioners likely to give the impression that the charity is connected in some way with Her Majesty's Government or any local authority, or with any other body of persons or any individual, when it is not so connected; or

    (e) the name of the charity is in the opinion of the Commissioners offensive;

and in this subsection any reference to the name of a charity is, in relation to a registered charity, a reference to the name by which it is registered.

(3) Any direction given by virtue of subsection (2)(a) above must be given within 12 months of the time when the registered name was entered in the register in respect of the charity.

(4) Any direction given under this section with respect to a charity shall be given to the charity trustees; and on receiving any such direction the charity trustees shall give effect to it notwithstanding anything in the trusts of the charity.

(5) Where the name of any charity is changed under this section, then (without prejudice to section 4(6)(b) of the 1960 Act (notification of changes in particulars of registered charity)) it shall be the duty of the charity trustees forthwith to notify the Commissioners of the charity's new name and of the date on which the change occurred.

(6) A change of name by a charity under this section does not affect any rights or obligations of the charity; and any legal proceedings that might have been continued or commenced by or against it in its former name may be continued or commenced by or against it in its new name.

1985 c.6.

(7) Section 26(3) of the Companies Act 1985 (minor variations in names to be disregarded) shall apply for the purposes of this section as if the reference to section 26(1)(c) of that Act were a reference to subsection (2)(a) above.

(8) Any reference in this section to the charity trustees of a charity shall, in relation to a charity which is a company, be read as a reference to the directors of the company.

(9) Nothing in this section applies to an exempt charity.

5.—(1) Where any direction is given under section 4 of this Act with respect to a charity which is a company, the direction shall be taken to require the name of the charity to be changed by resolution of the directors of the company.

(2) Section 380 of the Companies Act 1985 (registration etc. of resolutions and agreements) shall apply to any resolution passed by the directors in compliance with any such direction.

(3) Where the name of such a charity is changed in compliance with any such direction, the registrar of companies—

(a) shall (subject to section 26 of the Companies Act 1985 (prohibition on registration of certain names)) enter the new name on the register of companies in place of the former name, and

(b) shall issue a certificate of incorporation altered to meet the circumstances of the case;

and the change of name has effect from the date on which the altered certificate is issued.

Supervision and control by Commissioners

6.—(1) Section 6 of the 1960 Act (general power to institute inquiries) shall be amended as follows.

(2) In subsection (3)—

(a) for the words from "may by order" to "require" there shall be substituted ", or a person appointed by them to conduct it, may direct"; and

(b) for paragraph (b) there shall be substituted—

"(b) to furnish copies of documents in his custody or under his control which relate to any matter in question at the inquiry, and to verify any such copies by statutory declaration;

(c) to attend at a specified time and place and give evidence or produce any such documents."

(3) In subsection (5), for "an order or precept under paragraph (b)" there shall be substituted "a direction under paragraph (c)".

(4) Subsection (6) (exemption for person claiming to hold property adversely to a charity) shall be omitted.

(5) For subsection (7) there shall be substituted—

"(7) Where an inquiry has been held under this section, the Commissioners may either—

(a) cause the report of the person conducting the inquiry, or such other statement of the results of the inquiry as they think fit, to be printed and published, or

(b) publish any such report or statement in some other way which is calculated in their opinion to bring it to the attention of persons who may wish to make representations to them about the action to be taken."

(6) Subsection (9) (which is superseded by section 54(2) below) shall be omitted.

Power of
Commissioners to
obtain
information and
documents.

7.—(1) Section 7 of the 1960 Act (power to call for documents and search records) shall be amended as follows.

(2) For subsection (1) there shall be substituted—

"(1) The Commissioners may by order—

(a) require any person to furnish them with any information in his possession which relates to any charity and is relevant to the discharge of their functions or of the functions of the official custodian for charities;

(b) require any person who has in his custody or under his control any document which relates to any charity and is relevant to the discharge of their functions or of the functions of the official custodian for charities—

(i) to furnish them with a copy of or extract from the document, or

(ii) (unless the document forms part of the records or other documents of a court or of a public or local authority) to transmit the document itself to them for their inspection."

(3) Subsection (4) (exemption for person claiming to hold property adversely to a charity) shall be omitted.

(4) At the end of the section there shall be added—

"(6) The rights conferred by subsection (2) above shall, in relation to information recorded otherwise than in legible form, include the right to require the information to be made available in legible form for inspection or for a copy or extract to be made of or from it."

Power to act for
protection of
charities.

8.—(1) Section 20 of the 1960 Act (power to act for protection of charities) shall be amended as follows.

(2) For subsection (1) there shall be substituted—

"(1) Where, at any time after they have instituted an inquiry under section 6 of this Act with respect to any charity, the Commissioners are satisfied—

(a) that there is or has been any misconduct or mismanagement in the administration of the charity; or

(b) that it is necessary or desirable to act for the purpose of protecting the property of the charity or securing a proper application for the purposes of the charity of that property or of property coming to the charity;

the Commissioners may of their own motion do one or more of the following things, namely—

(i) by order suspend any trustee, charity trustee, officer, agent or employee of the charity from the exercise of his office or employment pending consideration being given to his removal (whether under this section or otherwise);

(ii) by order appoint such number of additional charity trustees as they consider necessary for the proper administration of the charity;

(iii) by order vest any property held by or in trust for the charity in the official custodian for charities, or require the persons in whom any such property is vested to transfer it to him, or appoint any person to transfer any such property to him;

(iv) order any person who holds any property on behalf of the charity, or of any trustee for it, not to part with the property without the approval of the Commissioners;

(v) order any debtor of the charity not to make any payment in or towards the discharge of his liability to the charity without the approval of the Commissioners;

(vi) by order restrict (notwithstanding anything in the trusts of the charity) the transactions which may be entered into, or the nature or amount of the payments which may be made, in the administration of the charity without the approval of the Commissioners;

(vii) by order appoint (in accordance with section 20A of this Act) a receiver and manager in respect of the property and affairs of the charity.

(1A) Where, at any time after they have instituted an inquiry under section 6 of this Act with respect to any charity, the Commissioners are satisfied—

(a) that there is or has been any misconduct or mismanagement in the administration of the charity; and

(b) that it is necessary or desirable to act for the purpose of protecting the property of the charity or securing a proper application for the purposes of the charity of that property or of property coming to the charity;

the Commissioners may of their own motion do either or both of the following things, namely—

(i) by order remove any trustee, charity trustee, officer, agent or employee of the charity who has been responsible for or privy to the misconduct or mismanagement or has by his conduct contributed to it or facilitated it;

(ii) by order establish a scheme for the administration of the charity."

(3) In subsection (2), after "subsection (1)" there shall be inserted "or (1A)".

(4) In subsection (3), for paragraph (a) there shall be substituted—

"(a) where, within the last five years, the trustee—

(i) having previously been adjudged bankrupt or had his estate sequestrated, has been discharged, or

(ii) having previously made a composition or arrangement with, or granted a trust deed for, his creditors, has been discharged in respect of it;

(aa) where the trustee is a corporation in liquidation;

(ab) where the trustee is incapable of acting by reason of mental disorder within the meaning of the Mental Health Act 1983;".

(5) For subsection (7) there shall be substituted—

"(7) Subject to subsection (7A) below, subsections (10) and (11) of section 18 of this Act shall apply to orders under this section as they apply to orders under that section.

(7A) The requirement to obtain any such certificate or leave as is mentioned in the proviso to section 18(11) shall not apply to—

(a) an appeal by a charity or any of the charity trustees of a charity against an order under subsection (1)(vii) above appointing a receiver and manager in respect of the charity's property and affairs, or

(b) an appeal by a person against an order under subsection (1A)(i) or (3)(a) above removing him from his office or employment.

(7B) Subsection (12) of section 18 of this Act shall apply to an order under this section which establishes a scheme for the administration of a charity as it applies to such an order under that section."

(6) In subsection (8), for the words from the beginning to "the suspension" there shall be substituted "The power of the Commissioners to make an order under subsection (1)(i) above shall not be exercisable so as to suspend any person from the exercise of his office or employment for a period of more than twelve months; but (without prejudice to the generality of section 40(1) of this Act) any such order made in the case of any person may make provision as respects the period of his suspension".

(7) In subsection (9), after "section" there shall be inserted "otherwise than by virtue of subsection (1) above".

(8) After subsection (9) there shall be inserted—

"(9A) The Commissioners shall, at such intervals as they think fit, review any order made by them under paragraph (i), or any of paragraphs (iii) to (vii), of subsection (1) above; and, if on any such review it appears to them that it would be appropriate to discharge the order in whole or in part, they shall so discharge it (whether subject to any savings or other transitional provisions or not)."

(9) For subsection (10) there shall be substituted—

"(10) If any person contravenes an order under subsection (1)(iv), (v) or (vi) above, he shall be guilty of an offence and liable on summary conviction to a fine not exceeding the fifth level on the standard scale.

(10A) Subsection (10) above shall not be taken to preclude the bringing of proceedings for breach of trust against any charity trustee or trustee for a charity in respect of a contravention of an order under subsection (1)(iv) or (vi) above (whether proceedings in respect of the contravention are brought against him under subsection (10) above or not)."

(10) Section 20 of the 1960 Act, as amended by this section, and with the omission of repealed provisions, is set out in Schedule 1 to this Act.

9. After section 20 of the 1960 Act there shall be inserted—

PART I
Supplementary
provisions
relating to receiver
and manager
appointed for a
charity.

"Supplementary provisions relating to receiver and manager appointed for a charity.

20A.—(1) The Commissioners may under section 20(1)(vii) of this Act appoint to be receiver and manager in respect of the property and affairs of a charity such person (other than an officer or employee of theirs) as they think fit.

(2) Without prejudice to the generality of section 40(1) of this Act, any order made by the Commissioners under section 20(1)(vii) of this Act may make provision with respect to the functions to be discharged by the receiver and manager appointed by the order; and those functions shall be discharged by him under the supervision of the Commissioners.

(3) In connection with the discharge of those functions any such order may provide—

    (a) for the receiver and manager appointed by the order to have such powers and duties of the charity trustees of the charity concerned (whether arising under this Act or otherwise) as are specified in the order;

    (b) for any powers or duties exercisable or falling to be performed by the receiver and manager by virtue of paragraph (a) above to be exercisable or performed by him to the exclusion of those trustees.

(4) Where a person has been appointed receiver and manager by any such order—

    (a) section 24 of this Act shall apply to him and to his functions as a person so appointed as it applies to a charity trustee of the charity concerned and to his duties as such; and

    (b) the Commissioners may apply to the High Court for directions in relation to any particular matter arising in connection with the discharge of those functions.

(5) The High Court may on an application under subsection (4)(b) above—

    (a) give such directions, or

    (b) make such orders declaring the rights of any persons (whether before the court or not),

as it thinks just; and the costs of any such application shall be paid by the charity concerned.

(6) Regulations may make provision with respect to—

    (a) the appointment and removal of persons appointed in accordance with this section;

    (b) the remuneration of such persons out of the income of the charities concerned;

    (c) the making of reports to the Commissioners by such persons.

(7) Regulations under subsection (6) above may, in particular, authorise the Commissioners—

(a) to require security for the due discharge of his functions to be given by a person so appointed;

(b) to determine the amount of such a person's remuneration;

(c) to disallow any amount of remuneration in such circumstances as are prescribed by the regulations."

Additional powers exercisable by Commissioners in relation to charitable companies.

10.—(1) At the end of section 30 of the 1960 Act (charitable companies: winding up) there shall be added—

"(2) Where a charity may be so wound up by the High Court, such a petition may also be presented by the Commissioners if, at any time after they have instituted an inquiry under section 6 of this Act with respect to the charity, they are satisfied as mentioned in section 20(1)(a) or (b) of this Act.

(3) Where a charitable company is dissolved, the Commissioners may make an application under section 651 of the Companies Act 1985 (power of court to declare dissolution of company void) for an order to be made under that section with respect to the company; and for this purpose subsection (1) of that section shall have effect in relation to a charitable company as if the reference to the liquidator of the company included a reference to the Commissioners.

(4) Where a charitable company's name has been struck off the register of companies under section 652 of the Companies Act 1985 (power of registrar to strike defunct company off register), the Commissioners may make an application under section 653(2) of that Act (objection to striking off by person aggrieved) for an order restoring the company's name to that register; and for this purpose section 653(2) shall have effect in relation to a charitable company as if the reference to any such person aggrieved as is there mentioned included a reference to the Commissioners.

(5) The powers exercisable by the Commissioners by virtue of this section shall be exercisable by them of their own motion, but shall be exercisable only with the agreement of the Attorney General on each occasion.

(6) In this section "charitable company" means a company which is a charity."

1989 c.40.

(2) The existing provisions of section 30 of the 1960 Act (as amended by the Companies Act 1989) shall accordingly constitute subsection (1) of that section.

Report of inquiry held by Commissioners to be evidence in certain proceedings.

11. After section 28 of the 1960 Act there shall be inserted—

"Report of s.6 inquiry to be evidence in certain proceedings.

28A.—(1) A copy of the report of the person conducting an inquiry under section 6 of this Act shall, if certified by the Commissioners to be a true copy, be admissible in any proceedings to which this section applies—

(a) as evidence of any fact stated in the report; and

(b) as evidence of the opinion of that person as to any matter referred to in it.

(2) This section applies to—

(a) any legal proceedings instituted by the Commissioners under this Part of this Act; and

(b) any legal proceedings instituted by the Attorney General in respect of a charity.

(3) A document purporting to be a certificate issued for the purposes of subsection (1) above shall be received in evidence and be deemed to be such a certificate, unless the contrary is proved."

12.—(1) The following provisions of the 1960 Act (as amended by this Act), namely—

(a) sections 6 and 7,

(b) section 20 (except subsection (1A)(ii)), and

(c) section 20A,

shall have effect in relation to any recognised body which is managed or controlled wholly or mainly in or from England or Wales as they have effect in relation to a charity; and in paragraph 3(6) of Schedule 1 to that Act (constitution etc. of Commissioners) the reference to sections 6, 20 and 20A of that Act includes a reference to those sections as applied by this subsection.

(2) Where—

(a) a recognised body is managed or controlled wholly or mainly in or from Scotland, but

(b) any person in England and Wales holds any property on behalf of the body or of any person concerned in its management or control,

then, if the Commissioners are satisfied as to the matters mentioned in subsection (3), they may make an order requiring the person holding the property not to part with it without their approval.

(3) The matters referred to in subsection (2) are—

(a) that there has been any misconduct or mismanagement in the administration of the body; and

(b) that it is necessary or desirable to make an order under that subsection for the purpose of protecting the property of the body or securing a proper application of such property for the purposes of the body;

and the reference in that subsection to the Commissioners being satisfied as to those matters is a reference to their being so satisfied on the basis of such information as may be supplied to them by the Lord Advocate.

(4) Where—

(a) any person in England and Wales holds any property on behalf of a recognised body or of any person concerned in the management or control of such a body, and

(b) the Commissioners are satisfied (whether on the basis of such information as may be supplied to them by the Lord Advocate or otherwise)—

> (i) that there has been any misconduct or mismanagement in the administration of the body, and

> (ii) that it is necessary or desirable to make an order under this subsection for the purpose of protecting the property of the body or securing a proper application of such property for the purposes of the body,

the Commissioners may by order vest the property in such recognised body or charity as is specified in the order in accordance with subsection (5), or require any persons in whom the property is vested to transfer it to any such body or charity, or appoint any person to transfer the property to any such body or charity.

(5) The Commissioners may specify in an order under subsection (4) such other recognised body or such charity as they consider appropriate, being a body or charity whose purposes are, in the opinion of the Commissioners, as similar in character to those of the body referred to in paragraph (a) of that subsection as is reasonably practicable; but the Commissioners shall not so specify any body or charity unless they have received—

(a) from the persons concerned in the management or control of the body, or

(b) from the charity trustees of the charity,

as the case may be, written confirmation that they are willing to accept the property.

(6) In this section "recognised body" has the same meaning as in Part I of the Law Reform (Miscellaneous Provisions) (Scotland) Act 1990 (Scottish charities).

1990 c.40.

Powers with respect to administration of charities

Commissioners' concurrent jurisdiction with High Court for certain purposes.

13.—(1) Section 18 of the 1960 Act (Commissioners' concurrent jurisdiction with High Court for certain purposes) shall be amended as follows.

(2) At the end of subsection (4) there shall be added "; or

(c) in the case of a charity other than an exempt charity, on the application of the Attorney General."

(3) For subsection (5) there shall be substituted—

"(5) In the case of a charity which is not an exempt charity and whose income from all sources does not in aggregate exceed £500 a year, the Commissioners may exercise their jurisdiction under this section on the application—

(a) of any one or more of the charity trustees; or

(b) of any person interested in the charity; or

(c) of any two or more inhabitants of the area of the charity, if it is a local charity."

(4) In subsection (6), for the words from "the Commissioners may" to "(5) above:" there shall be substituted "and the Commissioners have given the charity trustees an opportunity to make representations to them, the Commissioners may proceed as if an application for a scheme had been made by the charity:".

(5) After subsection (6) there shall be inserted—

"(6A) Where—

(a) a charity cannot apply to the Commissioners for a scheme by reason of any vacancy among the charity trustees or the absence or incapacity of any of them, but

(b) such an application is made by such number of the charity trustees as the Commissioners consider appropriate in the circumstances of the case,

the Commissioners may nevertheless proceed as if the application were an application made by the charity."

(6) At the end of the section there shall be added—

"(13) If he thinks it expedient to do so—

(a) in consequence of changes in the value of money, or

(b) with a view to increasing the number of charities in respect of which the Commissioners may exercise their jurisdiction under this section in accordance with subsection (5) above,

the Secretary of State may by order amend that subsection by substituting a different sum for the sum for the time being specified there.

(14) Any such order shall be made by statutory instrument subject to annulment in pursuance of a resolution of either House of Parliament."

14.—(1) After section 21 of the 1960 Act there shall be inserted—

Trust corporations appointed by Commissioners under 1960 Act.

"Application of provisions to trust corporations appointed under s.18 or 20.

21A. In the definition of "trust corporation" contained in the following provisions, namely—

(a) section 117(xxx) of the Settled Land Act 1925,

(b) section 68(18) of the Trustee Act 1925,

(c) section 205(xxviii) of the Law of Property Act 1925,

(d) section 55(xxvi) of the Administration of Estates Act 1925, and

(e) section 128 of the Supreme Court Act 1981,

the reference to a corporation appointed by the court in any particular case to be a trustee includes a reference to a corporation appointed by the Commissioners under this Act to be a trustee."

(2) The amendment made by subsection (1) above shall be deemed always to have had effect; but in the section 21A inserted by that subsection the reference to section 128 of the Supreme Court Act 1981 shall, in relation to any time before 1st January 1982, be construed as a reference to section 175(1) of the Supreme Court of Judicature (Consolidation) Act 1925.

1981 c.54.

1925 c.49.

15.—(1) Section 14 of the 1960 Act (application cy-près of gifts of donors unknown or disclaiming) shall be amended as follows.

(2) In subsection (1)—

(a) for "after such advertisements and inquiries as are reasonable, cannot" there shall be substituted "after—

(i) the prescribed advertisements and inquiries have been published and made, and

(ii) the prescribed period beginning with the publication of those advertisements has expired,

cannot"; and

(b) for "written disclaimer" there shall be inserted "disclaimer in the prescribed form".

(3) After subsection (1) there shall be inserted—

"(1A) Where the prescribed advertisements and inquiries have been published and made by or on behalf of trustees with respect to any such property, the trustees shall not be liable to any person in respect of the property if no claim by him to be interested in it is received by them before the expiry of the period mentioned in subsection (1)(a)(ii) above."

(4) In subsection (4)(b), for "twelve" there shall be substituted "six".

(5) After subsection (4) there shall be inserted—

"(4A) Where—

(a) any sum is, in accordance with any such directions, set aside for meeting any such claims, but

(b) the aggregate amount of any such claims actually made exceeds the relevant amount,

then, if the Commissioners so direct, each of the donors in question shall be entitled only to such proportion of the relevant amount as the amount of his claim bears to the aggregate amount referred to in paragraph (b) above; and for this purpose "the relevant amount" means the amount of the sum so set aside after deduction of any expenses properly incurred by the charity trustees in connection with claims relating to the donors' gifts."

(6) After subsection (5) there shall be inserted—

"(5A) In this section "prescribed" means prescribed by regulations made by the Commissioners; and such regulations may, as respects the advertisements which are to be published for the purposes of subsection (1)(a) above, make provision as to the form and content of such advertisements as well as the manner in which they are to be published.

(5B) Any regulations made by the Commissioners under this section shall be published by the Commissioners in such manner as they think fit."

16. After section 22 of the 1960 Act there shall be inserted—

"Schemes to establish common deposit funds.

22A.—(1) The court or the Commissioners may by order make and bring into effect schemes (in this section referred to as "common deposit schemes") for the establishment of common deposit funds under trusts which provide—

    (a) for sums to be deposited by or on behalf of a charity participating in the scheme and invested under the control of trustees appointed to manage the fund; and

    (b) for any such charity to be entitled (subject to the provisions of the scheme) to repayment of any sums so deposited and to interest thereon at a rate determined under the scheme.

(2) Subject to subsection (3) below, the following provisions of section 22 of this Act, namely—

    (a) subsections (2) to (4), and

    (b) subsections (7) to (11),

shall have effect in relation to common deposit schemes and common deposit funds as they have effect in relation to common investment schemes and common investment funds.

(3) In its application in accordance with subsection (2) above, subsection (4) of that section shall have effect with the substitution for paragraphs (b) and (c) of the following paragraphs—

    "(b) for regulating as to time, amount or otherwise the right to repayment of sums deposited in the fund;

    (c) for authorising a part of the income for any year to be credited to a reserve account maintained for the purpose of counteracting any losses accruing to the fund, and generally for regulating the manner in which the rate of interest on deposits is to be determined from time to time;"."

17. After section 23 of the 1960 Act there shall be inserted—

"Power to authorise certain ex gratia payments etc.

23A.—(1) Subject to subsection (3) below, the Commissioners may by order exercise the same power as is exercisable by the Attorney General to authorise the charity trustees of a charity—

    (a) to make any application of property of the charity, or

    (b) to waive to any extent, on behalf of the charity, its entitlement to receive any property,

in a case where the charity trustees—

    (i) (apart from this section) have no power to do so, but

(ii) in all the circumstances regard themselves as being under a moral obligation to do so.

(2) The power conferred on the Commissioners by subsection (1) above shall be exercisable by them under the supervision of, and in accordance with such directions as may be given by, the Attorney General; and any such directions may in particular require the Commissioners, in such circumstances as are specified in the directions—

(a) to refrain from exercising that power; or

(b) to consult the Attorney General before exercising it.

(3) Where—

(a) an application is made to the Commissioners for them to exercise that power in a case where they are not precluded from doing so by any such directions, but

(b) they consider that it would nevertheless be desirable for the application to be entertained by the Attorney General rather than by them,

they shall refer the application to the Attorney General.

(4) It is hereby declared that where, in the case of any application made to them as mentioned in subsection (3)(a) above, the Commissioners determine the application by refusing to authorise charity trustees to take any action falling within subsection (1)(a) or (b) above, that refusal shall not preclude the Attorney General, on an application subsequently made to him by the trustees, from authorising the trustees to take that action."

Dormant bank accounts of charities.

18.—(1) Where the Commissioners—

(a) are informed by a relevant institution—

(i) that it holds one or more accounts in the name of or on behalf of a particular charity ("the relevant charity"), and

(ii) that the account, or (if it so holds two or more accounts) each of the accounts, is dormant, and

(b) are unable, after making reasonable inquiries, to locate that charity or any of its trustees,

they may give a direction under subsection (2).

(2) A direction under this subsection is a direction which—

(a) requires the institution concerned to transfer the amount, or (as the case may be) the aggregate amount, standing to the credit of the relevant charity in the account or accounts in question to such other charity as is specified in the direction in accordance with subsection (3); or

(b) requires the institution concerned to transfer to each of two or more other charities so specified in the direction such part of that amount or aggregate amount as is there specified in relation to that charity.

(3) The Commissioners may specify in a direction under subsection (2) such other charity or charities as they consider appropriate, having regard, in a case where the purposes of the relevant charity are known to them, to those purposes and to the purposes of the other charity or charities; but the Commissioners shall not so specify any charity unless they have received from the charity trustees written confirmation that those trustees are willing to accept the amount proposed to be transferred to the charity.

(4) Any amount received by a charity by virtue of this section shall be received by the charity on terms that—

  (a) it shall be held and applied by the charity for the purposes of the charity, but

  (b) it shall, as property of the charity, nevertheless be subject to any restrictions on expenditure to which it was subject as property of the relevant charity.

(5) Where—

  (a) the Commissioners have been informed as mentioned in subsection (1)(a) by any relevant institution, and

  (b) before any transfer is made by the institution in pursuance of a direction under subsection (2), the institution has, by reason of any circumstances, cause to believe that the account, or (as the case may be) any of the accounts, held by it in the name of or on behalf of the relevant charity is no longer dormant,

the institution shall forthwith notify those circumstances in writing to the Commissioners; and, if it appears to the Commissioners that the account or accounts in question is or are no longer dormant, they shall revoke any direction under subsection (2) which has previously been given by them to the institution with respect to the relevant charity.

(6) The receipt of any charity trustees or trustee for a charity in respect of any amount received from a relevant institution by virtue of this section shall be a complete discharge of the institution in respect of that amount.

(7) No obligation as to secrecy or other restriction on disclosure (however imposed) shall preclude a relevant institution from disclosing any information to the Commissioners for the purpose of enabling them to discharge their functions under this section.

(8) For the purposes of this section—

  (a) an account is dormant if no transaction, other than—

    (i) a transaction consisting in a payment into the account, or

    (ii) a transaction which the institution holding the account has itself caused to be effected,

  has been effected in relation to the account within the period of five years immediately preceding the date when the Commissioners are informed as mentioned in paragraph (a) of subsection (1);

  (b) a "relevant institution" means—

    (i) the Bank of England;

    (ii) an institution which is authorised by the Bank of England to operate a deposit-taking business under Part I of the Banking Act 1987;

1987 c.22.

> (iii) a building society which is authorised by the Building Societies Commission under section 9 of the Building Societies Act 1986 to raise money from its members; or

> (iv) such other institution mentioned in Schedule 2 to the Banking Act 1987 as the Secretary of State may prescribe by regulations; and

> (c) references to the transfer of any amount to a charity are references to its transfer—

>> (i) to the charity trustees, or

>> (ii) to any trustee for the charity,

> as the charity trustees may determine (and any reference to any amount received by a charity shall be construed accordingly).

(9) For the purpose of determining the matters in respect of which any of the powers conferred by section 6 or 7 of the 1960 Act (power of Commissioners to institute inquiries or obtain information) may be exercised it shall be assumed that the Commissioners have no functions under this section in relation to accounts to which this subsection applies (with the result that, for example, a relevant institution shall not, in connection with the functions of the Commissioners under this section, be required under section 6(3)(a) of that Act to furnish any statements, or answer any questions or inquiries, with respect to any such accounts held by the institution).

This subsection applies to accounts which are dormant accounts by virtue of subsection (8)(a) above but would not be such accounts if sub-paragraph (i) of that provision were omitted.

(10) Subsection (1) shall not apply to any account held in the name of or on behalf of an exempt charity.

Charity accounts

19.—(1) The charity trustees of a charity shall ensure that accounting records are kept in respect of the charity which are sufficient to show and explain all the charity's transactions, and which are such as to—

(a) disclose at any time, with reasonable accuracy, the financial position of the charity at that time, and

(b) enable the trustees to ensure that, where any statements of accounts are prepared by them under section 20(1), those statements of accounts comply with the requirements of regulations under that provision.

(2) The accounting records shall in particular contain—

(a) entries showing from day to day all sums of money received and expended by the charity, and the matters in respect of which the receipt and expenditure takes place; and

(b) a record of the assets and liabilities of the charity.

(3) The charity trustees of a charity shall preserve any accounting records made for the purposes of this section in respect of the charity for at least six years from the end of the financial year of the charity in which they are made.

(4) Where a charity ceases to exist within the period of six years mentioned in subsection (3) as it applies to any accounting records, the obligation to preserve those records in accordance with that subsection shall continue to be discharged by the last charity trustees of the charity, unless the Commissioners consent in writing to the records being destroyed or otherwise disposed of.

(5) Nothing in this section applies to a charity which is a company.

20.—(1) The charity trustees of a charity shall (subject to subsection (3)) prepare in respect of each financial year of the charity a statement of accounts complying with such requirements as to its form and contents as may be prescribed by regulations made by the Secretary of State.

(2) Without prejudice to the generality of subsection (1), regulations under that subsection may make provision—

(a) for any such statement to be prepared in accordance with such methods and principles as are specified or referred to in the regulations;

(b) as to any information to be provided by way of notes to the accounts;

and regulations under that subsection may also make provision for determining the financial years of a charity for the purposes of this Part and any regulations made under it.

(3) Where a charity's gross income in any financial year does not exceed £25,000, the charity trustees may, in respect of that year, elect to prepare the following, namely—

(a) a receipts and payments account, and

(b) a statement of assets and liabilities,

instead of a statement of accounts under subsection (1).

(4) The charity trustees of a charity shall preserve—

(a) any statement of accounts prepared by them under subsection (1), or

(b) any account and statement prepared by them under subsection (3),

for at least six years from the end of the financial year to which any such statement relates or (as the case may be) to which any such account and statement relate.

(5) Subsection (4) of section 19 shall apply in relation to the preservation of any such statement or account and statement as it applies in relation to the preservation of any accounting records (the references to subsection (3) of that section being read as references to subsection (4) above).

(6) The Secretary of State may by order amend subsection (3) above by substituting a different sum for the sum for the time being specified there.

(7) Nothing in this section applies to a charity which is a company.

21.—(1) Subsection (2) applies to a financial year of a charity ("the relevant year") if the charity's gross income or total expenditure in any of the following, namely—

(a) the relevant year,

(b) the financial year of the charity immediately preceding the relevant year (if any), and

(c) the financial year of the charity immediately preceding the year specified in paragraph (b) (if any),

exceeds £100,000.

(2) If this subsection applies to a financial year of a charity, the accounts of the charity for that year shall be audited by a person who—

1989 c. 40.   (a) is, in accordance with section 25 of the Companies Act 1989 (eligibility for appointment), eligible for appointment as a company auditor, or

(b) is a member of a body for the time being specified in regulations under section 22 below and is under the rules of that body eligible for appointment as auditor of the charity.

(3) If subsection (2) does not apply to a financial year of a charity, then (subject to subsection (4)) the accounts of the charity for that year shall, at the election of the charity trustees, either—

(a) be examined by an independent examiner, that is to say an independent person who is reasonably believed by the trustees to have the requisite ability and practical experience to carry out a competent examination of the accounts, or

(b) be audited by such a person as is mentioned in subsection (2).

(4) Where it appears to the Commissioners—

(a) that subsection (2), or (as the case may be) subsection (3), has not been complied with in relation to a financial year of a charity within ten months from the end of that year, or

(b) that, although subsection (2) does not apply to a financial year of a charity, it would nevertheless be desirable for the accounts of the charity for that year to be audited by such a person as is mentioned in that subsection,

the Commissioners may by order require the accounts of the charity for that year to be audited by such a person as is mentioned in that subsection.

(5) If the Commissioners make an order under subsection (4) with respect to a charity, then unless—

(a) the order is made by virtue of paragraph (b) of that subsection, and

(b) the charity trustees themselves appoint an auditor in accordance with the order,

the auditor shall be a person appointed by the Commissioners.

(6) The expenses of any audit carried out by an auditor appointed by the Commissioners under subsection (5), including the auditor's remuneration, shall be recoverable by the Commissioners—

(a) from the charity trustees of the charity concerned, who shall be personally liable, jointly and severally, for those expenses; or

(b) to the extent that it appears to the Commissioners not to be practical to seek recovery of those expenses in accordance with paragraph (a), from the funds of the charity.

(7) The Commissioners may—

(a) give guidance to charity trustees in connection with the selection of a person for appointment as an independent examiner;

(b) give such directions as they think appropriate with respect to the carrying out of an examination in pursuance of subsection (3)(a);

and any such guidance or directions may either be of general application or apply to a particular charity only.

(8) The Secretary of State may by order amend subsection (1) by substituting a different sum for the sum for the time being specified there.

(9) Nothing in this section applies to a charity which is a company; but section 8(3) to (6) of the 1960 Act (power of Commissioners to require condition and accounts of charity to be investigated and audited) shall continue to apply to such a charity.

22.—(1) The Secretary of State may by regulations make provision—

Supplementary provisions relating to audits etc.

(a) specifying one or more bodies for the purposes of section 21(2)(b);

(b) with respect to the duties of an auditor carrying out an audit under section 21, including provision with respect to the making by him of a report on—

(i) the statement of accounts prepared for the financial year in question under section 20(1), or

(ii) the account and statement so prepared under section 20(3),

as the case may be;

(c) with respect to the making by an independent examiner of a report in respect of an examination carried out by him under section 21;

(d) conferring on such an auditor or on an independent examiner a right of access with respect to books, documents and other records (however kept) which relate to the charity concerned;

(e) entitling such an auditor or an independent examiner to require, in the case of a charity, information and explanations from past or present charity trustees or trustees for the charity, or from past or present officers or employees of the charity;

(f) enabling the Commissioners, in circumstances specified in the regulations, to dispense with the requirements of section 21(2) or (3) in the case of a particular charity or in the case of any particular financial year of a charity.

(2) If any person fails to afford an auditor or an independent examiner any facility to which he is entitled by virtue of subsection (1)(d) or (e), the Commissioners may by order give—

(a) to that person, or

(b) to the charity trustees for the time being of the charity concerned,

such directions as the Commissioners think appropriate for securing that the default is made good.

(3) Section 727 of the Companies Act 1985 (power of court to grant relief in certain cases) shall have effect in relation to an auditor or independent examiner appointed by a charity in pursuance of section 21 above as it has effect in relation to a person employed as auditor by a company within the meaning of that Act.

Annual reports.

23.—(1) The charity trustees of a charity shall prepare in respect of each financial year of the charity an annual report containing—

(a) such a report by the trustees on the activities of the charity during that year, and

(b) such other information relating to the charity or to its trustees or officers,

as may be prescribed by regulations made by the Secretary of State.

(2) Without prejudice to the generality of subsection (1), regulations under that subsection may make provision—

(a) for any such report as is mentioned in paragraph (a) of that subsection to be prepared in accordance with such principles as are specified or referred to in the regulations;

(b) enabling the Commissioners to dispense with any requirement prescribed by virtue of subsection (1)(b) in the case of a particular charity or a particular class of charities, or in the case of a particular financial year of a charity or of any class of charities.

(3) The annual report required to be prepared under this section in respect of any financial year of a charity shall be transmitted to the Commissioners by the charity trustees—

(a) within ten months from the end of that year, or

(b) within such longer period as the Commissioners may for any special reason allow in the case of that report.

(4) Subject to subsection (5), any such annual report shall have attached to it the statement of accounts prepared for the financial year in question under section 20(1) or (as the case may be) the account and statement so prepared under section 20(3), together with—

(a) where the accounts of the charity for that year have been audited under section 21, a copy of the report made by the auditor on that statement of accounts or (as the case may be) on that account and statement;

(b) where the accounts of the charity for that year have been examined under section 21, a copy of the report made by the independent examiner in respect of the examination carried out by him under that section.

(5) Subsection (4) does not apply to a charity which is a company, and any annual report transmitted by the charity trustees of such a charity under subsection (3) shall instead have attached to it a copy of the charity's annual accounts prepared for the financial year in question under Part VII of the Companies Act 1985, together with a copy of the auditors' report on those accounts.

(6) Any annual report transmitted to the Commissioners under subsection (3), together with the documents attached to it, shall be kept by the Commissioners for such period as they think fit.

24.—(1) Nothing in sections 19 to 23 applies to any exempt charity; but section 32(1) and (2) of the 1960 Act (general obligation to keep accounts) shall continue to apply to any such charity.

(2) Nothing in sections 21 to 23 applies to any charity which—

(a) falls within section 4(4)(c) of the 1960 Act (certain charities with an annual income not exceeding £1,000), and

(b) is not registered.

(3) Except in accordance with subsection (6) below, nothing in section 23 applies to any charity (other than an exempt charity or a charity which falls within section 4(4)(c) of the 1960 Act) which—

(a) is excepted by section 4(4) of that Act (charities not required to be registered), and

(b) is not registered.

(4) If requested to do so by the Commmissioners, the charity trustees of any such charity as is mentioned in subsection (3) above shall prepare an annual report in respect of such financial year of the charity as is specified in the Commissioners' request.

(5) Any report prepared under subsection (4) above shall contain—

(a) such a report by the charity trustees on the activities of the charity during the year in question, and

(b) such other information relating to the charity or to its trustees or officers,

as may be prescribed by regulations made under section 23(1) in relation to annual reports prepared under that provision.

(6) Subsections (3) to (6) of section 23 shall apply to any report required to be prepared under subsection (4) above as if it were an annual report required to be prepared under subsection (1) of that section.

(7) Any reference in this section to a charity which falls within section 4(4)(c) of the 1960 Act includes a reference to a charity which falls within that provision but is also excepted from registration by section 4(4)(b) of that Act (charities excepted by order or regulations).

25.—(1) Any annual report or other document kept by the Commissioners in pursuance of section 23(6) shall be open to public inspection at all reasonable times—

(a) during the period for which it is so kept; or

(b) if the Commissioners so determine, during such lesser period as they may specify.

(2) Section 9 of the 1960 Act (supply by Commissioners of copies of documents open to public inspection) shall have effect as if the reference to that Act included a reference to subsection (1) above.

(3) Where any person—

(a) requests the charity trustees of a charity in writing to provide him with a copy of the charity's most recent accounts, and

(b) pays them such reasonable fee (if any) as they may require in respect of the costs of complying with the request,

those trustees shall comply with the request within the period of two months beginning with the date on which it is made.

(4) In subsection (3) the reference to a charity's most recent accounts is—

(a) in the case of a charity other than one falling within any of paragraphs (b) to (d) below, a reference to the statement of accounts or account and statement prepared in pursuance of section 20(1) or (3) in respect of the last financial year of the charity the accounts for which have been audited or examined under section 21;

(b) in the case of such a charity as is mentioned in section 24(2), a reference to the statement of accounts or account and statement prepared in pursuance of section 20(1) or (3) in respect of the last financial year of the charity in respect of which a statement of accounts or account and statement has or have been so prepared;

(c) in the case of a charity which is a company, a reference to the annual accounts of the company most recently audited under Part VII of the Companies Act 1985; and

1985 c.6.

(d) in the case of an exempt charity, a reference to the accounts of the charity most recently audited in pursuance of any statutory or other requirement or, if its accounts are not required to be audited, the accounts most recently prepared in respect of the charity.

Annual returns by registered charities.

26.—(1) Every registered charity shall prepare in respect of each of its financial years an annual return in such form, and containing such information, as may be prescribed by regulations made by the Commissioners.

(2) Any such return shall be transmitted to the Commissioners by the date by which the charity trustees are, by virtue of section 23(3), required to transmit to them the annual report required to be prepared in respect of the financial year in question.

(3) The Commissioners may dispense with the requirements of subsection (1) in the case of a particular charity or a particular class of charities, or in the case of a particular financial year of a charity or of any class of charities.

Offences.

27. Any person who, without reasonable excuse, is persistently in default in relation to any requirement imposed—

(a) by section 23(3) (taken with section 23(4) or (5), as the case may require), or

(b) by section 25(3) or 26(2),

shall be guilty of an offence and liable on summary conviction to a fine not exceeding the fourth level on the standard scale.

Charity proceedings

28. After section 26 of the 1960 Act there shall be inserted—

26A.—(1) Subject to subsection (2) below, the Commissioners may exercise the same powers with respect to—

    (a) the taking of legal proceedings with reference to charities or the property or affairs of charities, or

    (b) the compromise of claims with a view to avoiding or ending such proceedings,

as are exercisable by the Attorney General acting ex officio.

(2) Subsection (1) above does not apply to the power of the Attorney General under section 30(1) of this Act to present a petition for the winding up of a charity.

(3) The practice and procedure to be followed in relation to any proceedings taken by the Commissioners under subsection (1) above shall be the same in all respects (and in particular as regards costs) as if they were proceedings taken by the Attorney General acting ex officio.

(4) No rule of law or practice shall be taken to require the Attorney General to be a party to any such proceedings.

(5) The powers exercisable by the Commissioners by virtue of this section shall be exercisable by them of their own motion, but shall be exercisable only with the agreement of the Attorney General on each occasion."

Charity property

29.—(1) The official custodian shall, in accordance with this section, divest himself of all property to which this subsection applies.

(2) Subsection (1) applies to any property held by the official custodian in his capacity as such, with the exception of—

    (a) any land; and

    (b) any property (other than land) which is vested in him by virtue of an order of the Commissioners under section 20 of the 1960 Act (power to act for protection of charities).

(3) Where property to which subsection (1) applies is held by the official custodian in trust for particular charities, he shall (subject to subsection (7)) divest himself of that property in such manner as the Commissioners may direct.

(4) Without prejudice to the generality of subsection (3), directions given by the Commissioners under that subsection may make different provision in relation to different property held by the official custodian or in relation to different classes or descriptions of property held by him, including (in particular)—

(a) provision designed to secure that the divestment required by subsection (1) is effected in stages or by means of transfers or other disposals taking place at different times;

(b) provision requiring the official custodian to transfer any specified investments, or any specified class or description of investments, held by him in trust for a charity—

    (i) to the charity trustees or any trustee for the charity, or

    (ii) to a person nominated by the charity trustees to hold any such investments in trust for the charity;

(c) provision requiring the official custodian to sell or call in any specified investments, or any specified class or description of investments, so held by him and to pay any proceeds of sale or other money accruing therefrom—

    (i) to the charity trustees or any trustee for the charity, or

    (ii) into any bank account kept in its name.

(5) The charity trustees of a charity may, in the case of any property falling to be transferred by the official custodian in accordance with a direction under subsection (3), nominate a person to hold any such property in trust for the charity; but a person shall not be so nominated unless—

(a) if an individual, he resides in England and Wales; or

(b) if a body corporate, it has a place of business there.

(6) Directions under subsection (3) shall, in the case of any property vested in the official custodian by virtue of section 22(6) of the 1960 Act (common investment funds), provide for any such property to be transferred—

(a) to the trustees appointed to manage the common investment fund concerned; or

(b) to any person nominated by those trustees who is authorised by or under the common investment scheme concerned to hold that fund or any part of it.

(7) Where the official custodian—

(a) holds any relevant property in trust for a charity, but

(b) after making reasonable inquiries is unable to locate the charity or any of its trustees,

he shall—

(i) unless the relevant property is money, sell the property and hold the proceeds of sale pending the giving by the Commissioners of a direction under subsection (8);

(ii) if the relevant property is money, hold it pending the giving of any such direction;

and for this purpose "relevant property" means any property to which subsection (1) applies or any proceeds of sale or other money accruing to the official custodian in consequence of a direction under subsection (3).

(8) Where subsection (7) applies in relation to a charity ("the dormant charity"), the Commissioners may direct the official custodian—

(a) to pay such amount as is held by him in accordance with that subsection to such other charity as is specified in the direction in accordance with subsection (9), or

(b) to pay to each of two or more other charities so specified in the direction such part of that amount as is there specified in relation to that charity.

(9) The Commissioners may specify in a direction under subsection (8) such charity or charities as they consider appropriate, being in each case a charity whose purposes are, in the opinion of the Commissioners, as similar in character to those of the dormant charity as is reasonably practicable; but the Commissioners shall not so specify any charity unless they have received from the charity trustees written confirmation that they are willing to accept the amount proposed to be paid to the charity.

(10) Any amount received by a charity by virtue of subsection (8) shall be received by the charity on terms that—

(a) it shall be held and applied by the charity for the purposes of the charity, but

(b) it shall, as property of the charity, nevertheless be subject to any restrictions on expenditure to which it, or (as the case may be) the property which it represents, was subject as property of the dormant charity.

(11) At such time as the Commissioners are satisfied that the official custodian has divested himself of all property held by him in trust for particular charities, all remaining funds held by him as official custodian shall be paid by him into the Consolidated Fund.

(12) Nothing in subsection (11) applies in relation to any property held by the official custodian which falls within subsection (2)(a) or (b).

(13) In this section "land" does not include any interest in land by way of mortgage or other security.

30.—(1) Any directions of the Commissioners under section 29 above shall have effect notwithstanding anything—

Provisions supplementary to s. 29.

(a) in the trusts of a charity, or

(b) in section 17(1) of the 1960 Act (supplementary provisions as to property vested in official custodian).

(2) Subject to subsection (3), any provision—

(a) of the trusts of a charity, or

(b) of any directions given by an order of the Commissioners made in connection with a transaction requiring the sanction of an order under section 29(1) of the 1960 Act (restrictions on dealing with charity property),

shall cease to have effect if and to the extent that it requires or authorises personal property of the charity to be transferred to or held by the official custodian; and for this purpose "personal property" extends to any mortgage or other real security, but does not include any interest in land other than such an interest by way of mortgage or other security.

(3) Subsection (2) does not apply to—

(a) any provision of an order made under section 20 of the 1960 Act (power to act for protection of charities); or

(b) any provision of any other order, or of any scheme, of the Commissioners if the provision requires trustees of a charity to make payments into an account maintained by the official custodian with a view to the accumulation of a sum as capital of the charity (whether or not by way of recoupment of a sum expended out of the charity's permanent endowment);

but any such provision as is mentioned in paragraph (b) shall have effect as if, instead of requiring the trustees to make such payments into an account maintained by the official custodian, it required the trustees to make such payments into an account maintained by them or by any other person (apart from the official custodian) who is either a trustee for the charity or a person nominated by them to hold such payments in trust for the charity.

(4) The disposal of any property by the official custodian in accordance with section 29 above shall operate to discharge him from his trusteeship of that property.

(5) Where any instrument issued by the official custodian in connection with any such disposal contains a printed reproduction of his official seal, that instrument shall have the same effect as if it were duly sealed with his official seal.

Divestment in the case of land subject to Reverter of Sites Act 1987.

31.—(1) Where—

(a) any land is vested in the official custodian in trust for a charity, and

(b) it appears to the Commissioners that section 1 of the 1987 Act (right of reverter replaced by trust for sale) will, or is likely to, operate in relation to the land at a particular time or in particular circumstances,

the jurisdiction which, under section 18 of the 1960 Act (Commissioners' concurrent jurisdiction with High Court for certain purposes), is exercisable by the Commissioners for the purpose of discharging a trustee for a charity may, at any time before section 1 of the 1987 Act operates in relation to the land, be exercised by them of their own motion for the purpose of—

(i) making an order discharging the official custodian from his trusteeship of the land, and

(ii) making such vesting orders and giving such directions as appear to them to be necessary or expedient in consequence.

(2) Where—

(a) section 1 of the 1987 Act has operated in relation to any land which, immediately before the time when that section so operated, was vested in the official custodian in trust for a charity, and

(b) the land remains vested in him but on the trust arising under that section,

the court or the Commissioners (of their own motion) may—

(i) make an order discharging the official custodian from his trusteeship of the land, and

(ii) (subject to the following provisions of this section) make such vesting orders and give such directions as appear to it or them to be necessary or expedient in consequence.

(3) Where any order discharging the official custodian from his trusteeship of any land—

(a) is made by the court under section 16(3) of the 1960 Act (discharge of official custodian), or by the Commissioners under section 18 of that Act, on the grounds that section 1 of the 1987 Act will, or is likely to, operate in relation to the land, or

(b) is made by the court or the Commissioners under subsection (2) above,

the persons in whom the land is to be vested on the discharge of the official custodian shall be the relevant charity trustees (as defined in subsection (4) below), unless the court or (as the case may be) the Commissioners is or are satisfied that it would be appropriate for it to be vested in some other persons.

(4) In subsection (3) above "the relevant charity trustees" means—

(a) in relation to an order made as mentioned in paragraph (a) of that subsection, the charity trustees of the charity in trust for which the land is vested in the official custodian immediately before the time when the order takes effect, or

(b) in relation to an order made under subsection (2) above, the charity trustees of the charity in trust for which the land was vested in the official custodian immediately before the time when section 1 of the 1987 Act operated in relation to the land.

(5) Where—

(a) section 1 of the 1987 Act has operated in relation to any such land as is mentioned in subsection (2)(a) above, and

(b) the land remains vested in the official custodian as mentioned in subsection (2)(b) above,

then (subject to subsection (6)), all the powers, duties and liabilities that would, apart from this section, be those of the official custodian as trustee for sale of the land shall instead be those of the charity trustees of the charity concerned; and those trustees shall have power in his name and on his behalf to execute and do all assurances and things which they could properly execute or do in their own name and on their own behalf if the land were vested in them.

(6) Subsection (5) shall not be taken to require or authorise those trustees to sell the land at a time when it remains vested in the official custodian.

(7) Where—

(a) the official custodian has been discharged from his trusteeship of any land by an order under subsection (2), and

(b) the land has, in accordance with subsection (3), been vested in the charity trustees concerned or (as the case may be) in any persons other than those trustees,

the land shall be held by those trustees, or (as the case may be) by those persons, as trustees for sale on the terms of the trust arising under section 1 of the 1987 Act.

(8) The official custodian shall not be liable to any person in respect of any loss or misapplication of any land vested in him in accordance with that section unless it is occasioned by or through any wilful neglect or default of his or of any person acting for him; but the Consolidated Fund shall be liable to make good to any person any sums for which the official custodian may be liable by reason of any such neglect or default.

(9) In this section—

1987 c.15.

(a) "the 1987 Act" means the Reverter of Sites Act 1987; and

(b) any reference to section 1 of the 1987 Act operating in relation to any land is a reference to a trust for sale arising in relation to the land under that section.

Restrictions on dispositions of charity land.

32.—(1) Subject to the following provisions of this section and section 37, no land held by or in trust for a charity shall be sold, leased or otherwise disposed of without an order of the court or of the Commissioners.

(2) Subsection (1) above shall not apply to a disposition of such land if—

(a) the disposition is made to a person who is not—

(i) a connected person (as defined in Schedule 2 to this Act), or

(ii) a trustee for, or nominee of, a connected person; and

(b) the requirements of subsection (3) or (5) below have been complied with in relation to it.

(3) Except where the proposed disposition is the granting of such a lease as is mentioned in subsection (5), the charity trustees must, before entering into an agreement for the sale, or (as the case may be) for a lease or other disposition, of the land—

(a) obtain and consider a written report on the proposed disposition from a qualified surveyor instructed by the trustees and acting exclusively for the charity;

(b) advertise the proposed disposition for such period and in such manner as the surveyor has advised in his report (unless he has there advised that it would not be in the best interests of the charity to advertise the proposed disposition); and

(c) decide that they are satisfied, having considered the surveyor's report, that the terms on which the disposition is proposed to be made are the best that can reasonably be obtained for the charity.

(4) For the purposes of subsection (3) a person is a qualified surveyor if—

    (a) he is a fellow or professional associate of the Royal Institution of Chartered Surveyors or of the Incorporated Society of Valuers and Auctioneers or satisfies such other requirement or requirements as may be prescribed by regulations made by the Secretary of State; and

    (b) he is reasonably believed by the charity trustees to have ability in, and experience of, the valuation of land of the particular kind, and in the particular area, in question;

and any report prepared for the purposes of that subsection shall contain such information, and deal with such matters, as may be prescribed by regulations so made.

(5) Where the proposed disposition is the granting of a lease for a term ending not more than seven years after it is granted (other than one granted wholly or partly in consideration of a fine), the charity trustees must, before entering into an agreement for the lease—

    (a) obtain and consider the advice on the proposed disposition of a person who is reasonably believed by the trustees to have the requisite ability and practical experience to provide them with competent advice on the proposed disposition; and

    (b) decide that they are satisfied, having considered that person's advice, that the terms on which the disposition is proposed to be made are the best that can reasonably be obtained for the charity.

(6) Where—

    (a) any land is held by or in trust for a charity, and

    (b) the trusts on which it is so held stipulate that it is to be used for the purposes, or any particular purposes, of the charity,

then (subject to subsections (7) and (8) and without prejudice to the operation of the preceding provisions of this section), the land shall not be sold, leased or otherwise disposed of unless the charity trustees have previously—

    (i) given public notice of the proposed disposition, inviting representations to be made to them within a time specified in the notice, being not less than one month from the date of the notice; and

    (ii) taken into consideration any representations made to them within that time about the proposed disposition.

(7) Subsection (6) shall not apply to any such disposition of land as is there mentioned if—

    (a) the disposition is to be effected with a view to acquiring by way of replacement other property which is to be held on the trusts referred to in paragraph (b) of that subsection; or

    (b) the disposition is the granting of a lease for a term ending not more than two years after it is granted (other than one granted wholly or partly in consideration of a fine).

(8) The Commissioners may direct—

    (a) that subsection (6) shall not apply to dispositions of land held by or in trust for a charity or class of charities (whether generally or only in the case of a specified class of dispositions or land, or otherwise as may be provided in the direction), or

    (b) that that subsection shall not apply to a particular disposition of land held by or in trust for a charity,

if, on an application made to them in writing by or on behalf of the charity or charities in question, the Commissioners are satisfied that it would be in the interests of the charity or charities for them to give the direction.

(9) The restrictions on disposition imposed by this section apply notwithstanding anything in the trusts of a charity; but nothing in this section applies—

    (a) to any disposition for which general or special authority is expressly given (without the authority being made subject to the sanction of an order of the court) by any statutory provision contained in or having effect under an Act of Parliament or by any scheme legally established; or

    (b) to any disposition of land held by or in trust for a charity which—

        (i) is made to another charity otherwise than for the best price that can reasonably be obtained, and

        (ii) is authorised to be so made by the trusts of the first-mentioned charity; or

    (c) to the granting, by or on behalf of a charity and in accordance with its trusts, of a lease to any beneficiary under those trusts where the lease—

        (i) is granted otherwise than for the best rent that can reasonably be obtained; and

        (ii) is intended to enable the demised premises to be occupied for the purposes, or any particular purposes, of the charity.

(10) Nothing in this section applies—

    (a) to any disposition of land held by or in trust for an exempt charity;

    (b) to any disposition of land by way of mortgage or other security; or

    (c) to any disposition of an advowson.

(11) In this section "land" means land in England or Wales.

Supplementary provisions relating to dispositions of charity land.

33.—(1) Any of the following instruments, namely—

    (a) any contract for the sale, or for a lease or other disposition, of land which is held by or in trust for a charity, and

    (b) any conveyance, transfer, lease or other instrument effecting a disposition of such land,

shall state—

    (i) that the land is held by or in trust for a charity,

(ii) whether the charity is an exempt charity and whether the disposition is one falling within paragraph (a), (b) or (c) of subsection (9) of section 32, and

(iii) if it is not an exempt charity and the disposition is not one falling within any of those paragraphs, that the land is land to which the restrictions on disposition imposed by that section apply.

(2) Where any land held by or in trust for a charity is sold, leased or otherwise disposed of by a disposition to which subsection (1) or (2) of section 32 applies, the charity trustees shall certify in the instrument by which the disposition is effected—

(a) (where subsection (1) of that section applies) that the disposition has been sanctioned by an order of the court or of the Commissioners (as the case may be), or

(b) (where subsection (2) of that section applies) that the charity trustees have power under the trusts of the charity to effect the disposition, and that they have complied with the provisions of that section so far as applicable to it.

(3) Where subsection (2) above has been complied with in relation to any disposition of land, then in favour of a person who (whether under the disposition or afterwards) acquires an interest in the land for money or money's worth, it shall be conclusively presumed that the facts were as stated in the certificate.

(4) Where—

(a) any land held by or in trust for a charity is sold, leased or otherwise disposed of by a disposition to which subsection (1) or (2) of section 32 applies, but

(b) subsection (2) above has not been complied with in relation to the disposition,

then in favour of a person who (whether under the disposition or afterwards) in good faith acquires an interest in the land for money or money's worth, the disposition shall be valid whether or not—

(i) (where subsection (1) of that section applies) the disposition has been sanctioned by an order of the court or of the Commissioners, or

(ii) (where subsection (2) of that section applies) the charity trustees have power under the trusts of the charity to effect the disposition and have complied with the provisions of that section so far as applicable to it.

(5) Any of the following instruments, namely—

(a) any contract for the sale, or for a lease or other disposition, of land which will, as a result of the disposition, be held by or in trust for a charity, and

(b) any conveyance, transfer, lease or other instrument effecting a disposition of such land,

shall state—

(i) that the land will, as a result of the disposition, be held by or in trust for a charity,

(ii) whether the charity is an exempt charity, and

(iii) if it is not an exempt charity, that the restrictions on disposition imposed by section 32 will apply to the land (subject to subsection (9) of that section).

(6) In section 29(1) of the Settled Land Act 1925 (charitable and public trusts)—

(a) the requirement for a conveyance of land held on charitable, ecclesiastical or public trusts to state that it is held on such trusts shall not apply to any instrument to which subsection (1) above applies; and

(b) the requirement imposed on a purchaser, in the circumstances mentioned in section 29(1) of that Act, to see that any consents or orders requisite for authorising a transaction have been obtained shall not apply in relation to any disposition in relation to which subsection (2) above has been complied with;

and expressions used in this subsection which are also used in that Act have the same meaning as in that Act.

(7) Where—

(a) the disposition to be effected by any such instrument as is mentioned in subsection (1)(b) or (5)(b) will be a registered disposition, or

(b) any such instrument will on taking effect be an instrument to which section 123(1) of the Land Registration Act 1925 (compulsory registration of title) applies,

the statement which, by virtue of subsection (1) or (5), is to be contained in the instrument shall be in such form as may be prescribed.

(8) Where—

(a) an application is duly made—

(i) for registration of a disposition of registered land, or

(ii) for registration of a person's title under a disposition of unregistered land, and

(b) the instrument by which the disposition is effected contains a statement complying with subsections (5) and (7) above, and

(c) the charity by or in trust for which the land is held as a result of the disposition is not an exempt charity,

the registrar shall enter in the register, in respect of the land, a restriction in such form as may be prescribed.

(9) Where—

(a) any such restriction is entered in the register in respect of any land, and

(b) the charity by or in trust for which the land is held becomes an exempt charity,

the charity trustees shall apply to the registrar for the restriction to be withdrawn; and on receiving any application duly made under this subsection the registrar shall withdraw the restriction.

(10) Where—

(a) any registered land is held by or in trust for an exempt charity and the charity ceases to be an exempt charity, or

(b) any registered land becomes, as a result of a declaration of trust by the registered proprietor, land held in trust for a charity (other than an exempt charity),

the charity trustees shall apply to the registrar for such a restriction as is mentioned in subsection (8) to be entered in the register in respect of the land; and on receiving any application duly made under this subsection the registrar shall enter such a restriction in the register in respect of the land.

(11) In this section—

(a) references to a disposition of land do not include references to—

(i) a disposition of land by way of mortgage or other security,

(ii) any disposition of an advowson, or

(iii) any release of a rentcharge falling within section 37(1); and

(b) "land" means land in England or Wales;

and subsections (7) to (10) above shall be construed as one with the Land Registration Act 1925.

1925 c.21.

34.—(1) Subject to subsection (2), no mortgage of land held by or in trust for a charity shall be granted without an order of the court or of the Commissioners.

Restrictions on mortgaging charity land.

(2) Subsection (1) shall not apply to a mortgage of any such land by way of security for the repayment of a loan where the charity trustees have, before executing the mortgage, obtained and considered proper advice, given to them in writing, on the matters mentioned in subsection (3).

(3) Those matters are—

(a) whether the proposed loan is necessary in order for the charity trustees to be able to pursue the particular course of action in connection with which the loan is sought by them;

(b) whether the terms of the proposed loan are reasonable having regard to the status of the charity as a prospective borrower; and

(c) the ability of the charity to repay on those terms the sum proposed to be borrowed.

(4) For the purposes of subsection (2) proper advice is the advice of a person—

(a) who is reasonably believed by the charity trustees to be qualified by his ability in and practical experience of financial matters; and

(b) who has no financial interest in the making of the loan in question;

and such advice may constitute proper advice for those purposes notwithstanding that the person giving it does so in the course of his employment as an officer or employee of the charity or of the charity trustees.

(5) This section applies notwithstanding anything in the trusts of a charity; but nothing in this section applies to any mortgage for which general or special authority is given as mentioned in section 32(9)(a).

(6) In this section—

"land" means land in England or Wales;

"mortgage" includes a charge.

(7) Nothing in this section applies to an exempt charity.

Supplementary provisions relating to mortgaging of charity land.

35.—(1) Any mortgage of land held by or in trust for a charity shall state—

(a) that the land is held by or in trust for a charity,

(b) whether the charity is an exempt charity and whether the mortgage is one falling within subsection (5) of section 34, and

(c) if it is not an exempt charity and the mortgage is not one falling within that subsection, that the mortgage is one to which the restrictions imposed by that section apply;

and where the mortgage will be a registered disposition any such statement shall be in such form as may be prescribed.

(2) Where subsection (1) or (2) of section 34 applies to any mortgage of land held by or in trust for a charity, the charity trustees shall certify in the mortgage—

(a) (where subsection (1) of that section applies) that the mortgage has been sanctioned by an order of the court or of the Commissioners (as the case may be), or

(b) (where subsection (2) of that section applies) that the charity trustees have power under the trusts of the charity to grant the mortgage, and that they have obtained and considered such advice as is mentioned in that subsection.

(3) Where subsection (2) above has been complied with in relation to any mortgage, then in favour of a person who (whether under the mortgage or afterwards) acquires an interest in the land in question for money or money's worth, it shall be conclusively presumed that the facts were as stated in the certificate.

(4) Where—

(a) subsection (1) or (2) of section 34 applies to any mortgage of land held by or in trust for a charity, but

(b) subsection (2) above has not been complied with in relation to the mortgage,

then in favour of a person who (whether under the mortgage or afterwards) in good faith acquires an interest in the land for money or money's worth, the mortgage shall be valid whether or not—

(i) (where subsection (1) of that section applies) the mortgage has been sanctioned by an order of the court or of the Commissioners, or

(ii) (where subsection (2) of that section applies) the charity trustees have power under the trusts of the charity to grant the mortgage and have obtained and considered such advice as is mentioned in that subsection.

(5) In section 29(1) of the Settled Land Act 1925 (charitable and public trusts)—

   (a) the requirement for a mortgage of land held on charitable, ecclesiastical or public trusts (as a "conveyance" of such land for the purposes of that Act) to state that it is held on such trusts shall not apply to any mortgage to which subsection (1) above applies; and

   (b) the requirement imposed on a mortgagee (as a "purchaser" for those purposes), in the circumstances mentioned in section 29(1) of that Act, to see that any consents or orders requisite for authorising a transaction have been obtained shall not apply in relation to any mortgage in relation to which subsection (2) above has been complied with;

and expressions used in this subsection which are also used in that Act have the same meaning as in that Act.

(6) In this section—

   "mortgage" includes a charge, and "mortgagee" shall be construed accordingly;

   "land" means land in England or Wales;

   "prescribed" and "registered disposition" have the same meaning as in the Land Registration Act 1925.

36.—(1) Any provision—

   (a) establishing or regulating a particular charity and contained in, or having effect under, any Act of Parliament, or

   (b) contained in the trusts of a charity,

shall cease to have effect if and to the extent that it provides for dispositions of, or other dealings with, land held by or in trust for the charity to require the consent of the Commissioners (whether signified by order or otherwise).

(2) Any provision of an order or scheme under the Education Act 1944 or the Education Act 1973 relating to a charity shall cease to have effect if and to the extent that it requires, in relation to any sale, lease or other disposition of land held by or in trust for the charity, approval by the Commissioners or the Secretary of State of the amount for which the land is to be sold, leased or otherwise disposed of.

(3) In this section "land" means land in England or Wales.

37.—(1) Section 32(1) shall not apply to the release by a charity of a rentcharge which it is entitled to receive if the release is given in consideration of the payment of an amount which is not less than ten times the annual amount of the rentcharge.

(2) Where a charity which is entitled to receive a rentcharge releases it in consideration of the payment of an amount not exceeding £500, any costs incurred by the charity in connection with proving its title to the rentcharge shall be recoverable by the charity from the person or persons in whose favour the rentcharge is being released.

(3) Neither section 32(1) nor subsection (2) above applies where a rentcharge which a charity is entitled to receive is redeemed under sections 8 to 10 of the Rentcharges Act 1977.

(4) The Secretary of State may by order amend subsection (2) above by substituting a different sum for the sum for the time being specified there.

(5) Subsections (2) to (8) of section 27 of the 1960 Act (special procedure for redemption of charity rentcharges) shall cease to have effect.

Powers of investment

Relaxation of restrictions on wider-range investments.

1961 c.62.

38.—(1) The Secretary of State may by order made with the consent of the Treasury—

(a) direct that, in the case of a trust fund consisting of property held by or in trust for a charity, any division of the fund in pursuance of section 2(1) of the Trustee Investments Act 1961 (trust funds to be divided so that wider-range and narrower-range investments are equal in value) shall be made so that the value of the wider-range part at the time of the division bears to the then value of the narrower-range part such proportion as is specified in the order;

(b) provide that, in its application in relation to such a trust fund, that Act shall have effect subject to such modifications so specified as the Secretary of State considers appropriate in consequence of, or in connection with, any such direction.

(2) Where, before the coming into force of an order under this section, a trust fund consisting of property held by or in trust for a charity has already been divided in pursuance of section 2(1) of that Act, the fund may, notwithstanding anything in that provision, be again divided (once only) in pursuance of that provision during the continuance in force of the order.

(3) No order shall be made under this section unless a draft of the order has been laid before and approved by a resolution of each House of Parliament.

(4) Expressions used in this section which are also used in the Trustee Investments Act 1961 have the same meaning as in that Act.

1990 c.40.

(5) In the application of this section to Scotland, "charity" means a recognised body within the meaning of section 1(7) of the Law Reform (Miscellaneous Provisions) (Scotland) Act 1990.

Extension of powers of investment.

1961 c.62.

39.—(1) The Secretary of State may by regulations made with the consent of the Treasury make, with respect to property held by or in trust for a charity, provision authorising a trustee to invest such property in any manner specified in the regulations, being a manner of investment not for the time being included in any Part of Schedule 1 to the Trustee Investments Act 1961.

(2) Regulations under this section may make such provision—

(a) regulating the investment of property in any manner authorised by virtue of subsection (1), and

(b) with respect to the variation and retention of investments so made,

as the Secretary of State considers appropriate.

(3) Such regulations may, in particular, make provision—

(a) imposing restrictions with respect to the proportion of the property held by or in trust for a charity which may be invested in any manner authorised by virtue of subsection (1), being either restrictions applying to investment in any such manner generally or restrictions applying to investment in any particular such manner;

(b) imposing the like requirements with respect to the obtaining and consideration of advice as are imposed by any of the provisions of section 6 of the Trustee Investments Act 1961 (duty of trustees in choosing investments).

1961 c.62.

(4) Any power of investment conferred by any regulations under this section—

(a) shall be in addition to, and not in derogation from, any power conferred otherwise than by such regulations; and

(b) shall not be limited by the trusts of a charity (in so far as they are not contained in any Act or instrument made under an enactment) unless it is excluded by those trusts in express terms;

but any such power shall only be exercisable by a trustee in so far as a contrary intention is not expressed in any Act or in any instrument made under an enactment and relating to the powers of the trustee.

(5) No regulations shall be made under this section unless a draft of the regulations has been laid before and approved by a resolution of each House of Parliament.

(6) In this section "property"—

(a) in England and Wales, means real or personal property of any description, including money and things in action, but does not include an interest in expectancy; and

(b) in Scotland, means property of any description (whether heritable or moveable, corporeal or incorporeal) which is presently enjoyable, but does not include a future interest, whether vested or contingent;

and any reference to property held by or in trust for a charity is a reference to property so held, whether it is for the time being in a state of investment or not.

(7) In the application of this section to Scotland, "charity" means a recognised body within the meaning of section 1(7) of the Law Reform (Miscellaneous Provisions) (Scotland) Act 1990.

1990 c.40.

Charitable companies

40. For subsections (2) and (3) of section 30A of the 1960 Act (as amended by the Companies Act 1989) there shall be substituted—

Charitable companies: alteration of objects clause etc. 1989 c.40.

"(2) Where a charity is a company, any alteration by it—

(a) of the objects clause in its memorandum of association, or

(b) of any other provision in its memorandum of association, or any provision in its articles of association, which is a provision directing or restricting the manner in which property of the company may be used or applied,

is ineffective without the prior written consent of the Commissioners.

(3) Where a company has made any such alteration in accordance with subsection (2) above and—

(a) in connection with the alteration is required by virtue of—

(i) section 6(1) of the Companies Act 1985 (delivery of documents following alteration of objects), or

(ii) that provision as applied by section 17(3) of that Act (alteration of condition in memorandum which could have been contained in articles),

to deliver to the registrar of companies a printed copy of its memorandum, as altered, or

(b) is required by virtue of section 380(1) of that Act (registration etc. of resolutions and agreements) to forward to the registrar a printed or other copy of the special resolution effecting the alteration,

the copy so delivered or forwarded by the company shall be accompanied by a copy of the Commissioners' consent.

(4) Section 6(3) of that Act (offences) shall apply to any default by a company in complying with subsection (3) above as it applies to any such default as is mentioned in that provision."

Charitable
companies:
requirement of
consent of
Commissioners to
certain acts.
1989 c.40.

41. After section 30B of the 1960 Act (as amended by the Companies Act 1989) there shall be inserted—

"Charitable
companies:
requirement of
consent of
Commissioners
to certain acts.

30BA.—(1) Where a company is a charity—

(a) any approval given by the company for the purposes of any of the provisions of the Companies Act 1985 specified in subsection (2) below, and

(b) any affirmation by it for the purposes of section 322(2)(c) of that Act (affirmation of voidable arrangements under which assets are acquired by or from a director or person connected with him),

is ineffective without the prior written consent of the Commissioners.

(2) The provisions of the Companies Act 1985 referred to in subsection (1)(a) above are—

(a) section 312 (payment to director in respect of loss of office or retirement);

(b) section 313(1) (payment to director in respect of loss of office or retirement made in connection with transfer of undertaking or property of company);

      (c) section 319(3) (incorporation in director's service contract of term whereby his employment will or may continue for a period of more than 5 years);

      (d) section 320(1) (arrangement whereby assets are acquired by or from director or person connected with him);

      (e) section 337(3)(a) (provision of funds to meet certain expenses incurred by director)."

42. The following section shall be inserted in the 1960 Act after the section 30BA inserted by section 41 above—

Charitable companies: name to appear on correspondence etc.

"Charitable companies: name to appear on correspondence etc.

      30BB. Section 30(7) of the Companies Act 1985 (exemption from requirements relating to publication of name etc.) shall not, in its application to any company which is a charity, have the effect of exempting the company from the requirements of section 349(1) of that Act (company's name to appear in its correspondence etc.)."

Small charities

43.—(1) This section applies to a charity if—

Small charities: power to transfer all property, modify objects etc.

      (a) its gross income in its last financial year did not exceed £5,000, and

      (b) it does not hold any land on trusts which stipulate that the land is to be used for the purposes, or any particular purposes, of the charity,

and it is neither an exempt charity nor a charitable company.

(2) Subject to the following provisions of this section, the charity trustees of a charity to which this section applies may resolve for the purposes of this section—

      (a) that all the property of the charity should be transferred to such other charity as is specified in the resolution, being either a registered charity or a charity which is not required to be registered;

      (b) that all the property of the charity should be divided, in such manner as is specified in the resolution, between such two or more other charities as are so specified, being in each case either a registered charity or a charity which is not required to be registered;

      (c) that the trusts of the charity should be modified by replacing all or any of the purposes of the charity with such other purposes, being in law charitable, as are specified in the resolution;

      (d) that any provision of the trusts of the charity—

          (i) relating to any of the powers exercisable by the charity trustees in the administration of the charity, or

          (ii) regulating the procedure to be followed in any respect in connection with its administration,

      should be modified in such manner as is specified in the resolution.

(3) Any resolution passed under subsection (2) must be passed by a majority of not less than two-thirds of such charity trustees as vote on the resolution.

(4) The charity trustees of a charity to which this section applies ("the transferor charity") shall not have power to pass a resolution under subsection (2)(a) or (b) unless they are satisfied—

    (a) that the existing purposes of the transferor charity have ceased to be conducive to a suitable and effective application of the charity's resources; and

    (b) that the purposes of the charity or charities specified in the resolution are as similar in character to the purposes of the transferor charity as is reasonably practicable;

and before passing the resolution they must have received from the charity trustees of the charity, or (as the case may be) of each of the charities, specified in the resolution written confirmation that those trustees are willing to accept a transfer of property under this section.

(5) The charity trustees of any such charity shall not have power to pass a resolution under subsection (2)(c) unless they are satisfied—

    (a) that the existing purposes of the charity (or, as the case may be, such of them as it is proposed to replace) have ceased to be conducive to a suitable and effective application of the charity's resources; and

    (b) that the purposes specified in the resolution are as similar in character to those existing purposes as is practical in the circumstances.

(6) Where charity trustees have passed a resolution under subsection (2), they shall—

    (a) give public notice of the resolution in such manner as they think reasonable in the circumstances; and

    (b) send a copy of the resolution to the Commissioners, together with a statement of their reasons for passing it.

(7) The Commissioners may, when considering the resolution, require the charity trustees to provide additional information or explanation—

    (a) as to the circumstances in and by reference to which they have determined to act under this section, or

    (b) relating to their compliance with this section in connection with the resolution;

and the Commissioners shall take into account any representations made to them by persons appearing to them to be interested in the charity where those representations are made within the period of six weeks beginning with the date when the Commissioners receive a copy of the resolution by virtue of subsection (6)(b).

(8) Where the Commissioners have so received a copy of a resolution from any charity trustees and it appears to them that the trustees have complied with this section in connection with the resolution, the Commissioners shall, within the period of three months beginning with the date when they receive the copy of the resolution, notify the trustees in writing either—

(a) that the Commissioners concur with the resolution; or

(b) that they do not concur with it.

(9) Where the Commissioners so notify their concurrence with the resolution, then—

(a) if the resolution was passed under subsection (2)(a) or (b), the charity trustees shall arrange for all the property of the transferor charity to be transferred in accordance with the resolution and on terms that any property so transferred—

(i) shall be held and applied by the charity to which it is transferred ("the transferee charity") for the purposes of that charity, but

(ii) shall, as property of the transferee charity, nevertheless be subject to any restrictions on expenditure to which it is subject as property of the transferor charity,

and those trustees shall arrange for it to be so transferred by such date as may be specified in the notification; and

(b) if the resolution was passed under subsection (2)(c) or (d), the trusts of the charity shall be deemed, as from such date as may be specified in the notification, to have been modified in accordance with the terms of the resolution.

(10) For the purpose of enabling any property to be transferred to a charity under this section, the Commissioners shall have power, at the request of the charity trustees of that charity, to make orders vesting any property of the transferor charity—

(a) in the charity trustees of the first-mentioned charity or in any trustee for that charity, or

(b) in any other person nominated by those charity trustees to hold the property in trust for that charity.

(11) The Secretary of State may by order amend subsection (1) by substituting a different sum for the sum for the time being specified there.

(12) In this section—

(a) "charitable company" means a charity which is a company or other body corporate; and

(b) references to the transfer of property to a charity are references to its transfer—

(i) to the charity trustees, or

(ii) to any trustee for the charity, or

(iii) to a person nominated by the charity trustees to hold it in trust for the charity,

as the charity trustees may determine.

44.—(1) This section applies to a charity if—

Small charities: power to spend capital.

(a) it has a permanent endowment which does not consist of or comprise any land, and

(b) its gross income in its last financial year did not exceed £1,000,

and it is neither an exempt charity nor a charitable company.

(2) Where the charity trustees of a charity to which this section applies are of the opinion that the property of the charity is too small, in relation to its purposes, for any useful purpose to be achieved by the expenditure of income alone, they may resolve for the purposes of this section that the charity ought to be freed from the restrictions with respect to expenditure of capital to which its permanent endowment is subject.

(3) Any resolution passed under subsection (2) must be passed by a majority of not less than two-thirds of such charity trustees as vote on the resolution.

(4) Before passing such a resolution the charity trustees must consider whether any reasonable possibility exists of effecting a transfer or division of all the charity's property under section 43 (disregarding any such transfer or division as would, in their opinion, impose on the charity an unacceptable burden of costs).

(5) Where charity trustees have passed a resolution under subsection (2), they shall—

    (a) give public notice of the resolution in such manner as they think reasonable in the circumstances; and

    (b) send a copy of the resolution to the Commissioners, together with a statement of their reasons for passing it.

(6) The Commissioners may, when considering the resolution, require the charity trustees to provide additional information or explanation—

    (a) as to the circumstances in and by reference to which they have determined to act under this section, or

    (b) relating to their compliance with this section in connection with the resolution;

and the Commissioners shall take into account any representations made to them by persons appearing to them to be interested in the charity where those representations are made within the period of six weeks beginning with the date when the Commissioners receive a copy of the resolution by virtue of subsection (5)(b).

(7) Where the Commissioners have so received a copy of a resolution from any charity trustees and it appears to them that the trustees have complied with this section in connection with the resolution, the Commissioners shall, within the period of three months beginning with the date when they receive the copy of the resolution, notify the trustees in writing either—

    (a) that the Commissioners concur with the resolution; or

    (b) that they do not concur with it.

(8) Where the Commissioners so notify their concurrence with the resolution, the charity trustees shall have, as from such date as may be specified in the notification, power by virtue of this section to expend any property of the charity without regard to any such restrictions as are mentioned in subsection (2).

(9) The Secretary of State may by order amend subsection (1) by substituting a different sum for the sum for the time being specified there.

(10) In this section "charitable company" means a charity which is a company or other body corporate.

Disqualification for acting as charity trustee

45.—(1) Subject to the following provisions of this section, a person shall be disqualified for being a charity trustee or trustee for a charity if—

  (a) he has been convicted of any offence involving dishonesty or deception;

  (b) he has been adjudged bankrupt or sequestration of his estate has been awarded and (in either case) he has not been discharged;

  (c) he has made a composition or arrangement with, or granted a trust deed for, his creditors and has not been discharged in respect of it;

  (d) he has been removed from the office of charity trustee or trustee for a charity by an order made—

    (i) by the Commissioners under section 20(1A)(i) of the 1960 Act (power to act for protection of charities) or under section 20(1)(i) of that Act (as in force before the commencement of section 8 of this Act), or

    (ii) by the High Court,

on the grounds of any misconduct or mismanagement in the administration of the charity for which he was responsible or to which he was privy, or which he by his conduct contributed to or facilitated;

  (e) he has been removed, under section 7 of the Law Reform (Miscellaneous Provisions) (Scotland) Act 1990 (powers of Court of Session to deal with management of charities), from being concerned in the management or control of any body;

  (f) he is subject to a disqualification order under the Company Directors Disqualification Act 1986 or to an order made under section 429(2)(b) of the Insolvency Act 1986 (failure to pay under county court administration order).

(2) In subsection (1)—

  (a) paragraph (a) applies whether the conviction occurred before or after the commencement of that subsection, but does not apply in relation to any conviction which is a spent conviction for the purposes of the Rehabilitation of Offenders Act 1974;

  (b) paragraph (b) applies whether the adjudication of bankruptcy or the sequestration occurred before or after the commencement of that subsection;

  (c) paragraph (c) applies whether the composition or arrangement was made, or the trust deed was granted, before or after the commencement of that subsection; and

  (d) paragraphs (d) to (f) apply in relation to orders made and removals effected before or after the commencement of that subsection.

(3) Where (apart from this subsection) a person is disqualified under subsection (1)(b) for being a charity trustee or trustee for any charity which is a company, he shall not be so disqualified if leave has been granted under section 11 of the Company Directors Disqualification Act 1986 (undischarged bankrupts) for him to act as director of the charity; and similarly a person shall not be disqualified under subsection (1)(f) for being a charity trustee or trustee for such a charity if—

Persons disqualified for being trustees of a charity.

1990 c.40.

1986 c.46.

1986 c.45.

1974 c.53.

(a) in the case of a person subject to a disqualification order, leave under the order has been granted for him to act as director of the charity, or

1986 c.45.

(b) in the case of a person subject to an order under section 429(2)(b) of the Insolvency Act 1986, leave has been granted by the court which made the order for him to so act.

(4) The Commissioners may, on the application of any person disqualified under subsection (1), waive his disqualification either generally or in relation to a particular charity or a particular class of charities; but no such waiver may be granted in relation to any charity which is a company if—

(a) the person concerned is for the time being prohibited, by virtue of—

1986 c.46.

(i) a disqualification order under the Company Directors Disqualification Act 1986, or

(ii) section 11(1) or 12(2) of that Act (undischarged bankrupts; failure to pay under county court administration order),

from acting as director of the charity; and

(b) leave has not been granted for him to act as director of any other company.

1978 c.30.

(5) Without prejudice to the generality of section 13 of the Interpretation Act 1978 (anticipatory exercise of powers), the Commissioners may—

(a) at any time before the commencement of subsection (1) above, and

(b) on the application of a person who would be disqualified under that subsection as from that commencement,

grant that person a waiver under subsection (4) taking effect as from that commencement.

(6) Any waiver under subsection (4) shall be notified in writing to the person concerned.

(7) For the purposes of this section the Commissioners shall keep, in such manner as they think fit, a register of all persons who have been removed from office as mentioned in subsection (1)(d) either—

(a) by an order of the Commissioners made before or after the commencement of subsection (1), or

(b) by an order of the High Court made after the commencement of that subsection;

and, where any person is so removed from office by an order of the High Court, the court shall notify the Commissioners of his removal.

(8) The entries in the register kept under subsection (7) shall be available for public inspection in legible form at all reasonable times.

Person acting as charity trustee while disqualified.

46.—(1) Subject to subsection (2), any person who acts as a charity trustee or trustee for a charity while he is disqualified for being such a trustee by virtue of section 45 shall be guilty of an offence and liable—

(a) on summary conviction, to imprisonment for a term not exceeding six months or to a fine not exceeding the statutory maximum, or both;

(b) on conviction on indictment, to imprisonment for a term not exceeding two years or to a fine, or both.

(2) Subsection (1) shall not apply where—

(a) the charity concerned is a company; and

(b) the disqualified person is disqualified by virtue only of paragraph (b) or (f) of section 45(1).

(3) Any acts done as charity trustee or trustee for a charity by a person disqualified for being such a trustee by virtue of section 45 shall not be invalid by reason only of that disqualification.

(4) Where the Commissioners are satisfied—

(a) that any person has acted as charity trustee or trustee for a charity (other than an exempt charity) while disqualified for being such a trustee by virtue of section 45, and

(b) that, while so acting, he has received from the charity any sums by way of remuneration or expenses, or any benefit in kind, in connection with his acting as charity trustee or trustee for the charity,

they may by order direct him to repay to the charity the whole or part of any such sums, or (as the case may be) to pay to the charity the whole or part of the monetary value (as determined by them) of any such benefit.

(5) Subsection (4) does not apply to any sums received by way of remuneration or expenses in respect of any time when the person concerned was not disqualified for being a charity trustee or trustee for the charity.

Miscellaneous and supplementary

47. The 1960 Act shall have effect subject to the amendments specified in Schedule 3 to this Act (which are either minor amendments or amendments consequential on the preceding provisions of this Part of this Act).

Minor and consequential amendments of 1960 Act.

48. The Charitable Trustees Incorporation Act 1872 shall have effect subject to the amendments specified in Schedule 4 to this Act.

Amendment of Charitable Trustees Incorporation Act 1872.
1872 c.24.

49. The Redundant Churches and Other Religious Buildings Act 1969 shall have effect subject to the amendments specified in Schedule 5 to this Act.

Amendment of Redundant Churches and Other Religious Buildings Act 1969.
1969 c.22.

PART I

Contributions towards maintenance etc. of almshouses.

50.—(1) Any provision in the trusts of an almshouse charity which relates to the payment by persons resident in the charity's almshouses of contributions towards the cost of maintaining those almshouses and essential services in them shall cease to have effect if and to the extent that it provides for the amount, or the maximum amount, of such contributions to be a sum specified, approved or authorised by the Commissioners.

(2) In subsection (1)—

"almshouse" means any premises maintained as an almshouse, whether they are called an almshouse or not; and

"almshouse charity" means a charity which is authorised under its trusts to maintain almshouses.

Fees and other amounts payable to Commissioners.

51.—(1) The Secretary of State may by regulations require the payment to the Commissioners of such fees as may be prescribed in respect of—

(a) the discharge by the Commissioners of such functions under the enactments relating to charities as may be prescribed;

(b) the inspection of the register of charities or of other material kept by them under those enactments, or the furnishing of copies of or extracts from documents so kept.

(2) Regulations under this section may—

(a) confer, or provide for the conferring of, exemptions from liability to pay a prescribed fee;

(b) provide for the remission or refunding of a prescribed fee (in whole or in part) in prescribed circumstances.

(3) A statutory instrument containing any regulations under this section which require the payment of a fee in respect of any matter for which no fee was previously payable shall not be made unless a draft of the regulations has been laid before and approved by a resolution of each House of Parliament.

(4) The Commissioners may impose charges of such amounts as they consider reasonable in respect of the supply of any publications produced by them.

(5) Any fees and other payments received by the Commissioners by virtue of this section shall be paid into the Consolidated Fund.

(6) In this section "prescribed" means prescribed by regulations under this section.

Disclosure of information to and by Commissioners.

52.—(1) Subject to subsection (2) and to any express restriction imposed by or under any other enactment, a body or person to whom this section applies may disclose to the Charity Commissioners any information received by that body or person under or for the purposes of any enactment, where the disclosure is made by the body or person for the purpose of enabling or assisting the Commissioners to discharge any of their functions.

(2) Subsection (1) shall not have effect in relation to the Commissioners of Customs and Excise or the Commissioners of Inland Revenue; but either of those bodies of Commissioners ("the relevant body") may disclose to the Charity Commissioners the following information, namely—

(a) the name and address of any institution which has for any purpose been treated by the relevant body as established for charitable purposes;

(b) information as to the purposes of an institution and the trusts under which it is established or regulated, where the disclosure is made by the relevant body in order to give or obtain assistance in determining whether the institution ought for any purpose to be treated as established for charitable purposes; and

(c) information with respect to an institution which has for any purpose been treated as so established but which appears to the relevant body—

   (i) to be, or to have been, carrying on activities which are not charitable, or

   (ii) to be, or to have been, applying any of its funds for purposes which are not charitable.

(3) In subsection (2) any reference to an institution shall, in relation to the Commissioners of Inland Revenue, be construed as a reference to an institution in England and Wales.

(4) Subject to subsection (5), the Charity Commissioners may disclose to a body or person to whom this section applies any information received by them under or for the purposes of any enactment, where the disclosure is made by the Commissioners—

(a) for any purpose connected with the discharge of their functions, and

(b) for the purpose of enabling or assisting that body or person to discharge any of its or his functions.

(5) Where any information disclosed to the Charity Commissioners under subsection (1) or (2) is so disclosed subject to any express restriction on the disclosure of the information by the Commissioners, the Commissioners' power of disclosure under subsection (4) shall, in relation to the information, be exercisable by them subject to any such restriction.

(6) This section applies to the following bodies and persons—

(a) any government department (including a Northern Ireland department);

(b) any local authority;

(c) any constable; and

(d) any other body or person discharging functions of a public nature (including a body or person discharging regulatory functions in relation to any description of activities).

(7) In subsection (6)(d) the reference to any such body or person as is there mentioned shall, in relation to a disclosure by the Charity Commissioners under subsection (4), be construed as including a reference to any such body or person in a country or territory outside the United Kingdom.

(8) Nothing in this section shall be construed as affecting any power of disclosure exercisable apart from this section.

(9) In this section "enactment" includes an enactment comprised in subordinate legislation (within the meaning of the Interpretation Act 1978).

1978 c.30.

53. An order under section 30 of the Data Protection Act 1984 (exemption from subject access provisions of data held for the purpose of discharging designated functions in connection with the regulation of financial services etc.) may designate for the purposes of that section, as if they were functions conferred by or under such an enactment as is there mentioned, any functions of the Commissioners appearing to the Secretary of State to be—

(a) connected with the protection of charities against misconduct or mismanagement (whether by trustees or other persons) in their administration; or

(b) connected with the protection of the property of charities from loss or misapplication or with the recovery of such property.

Supply of false or misleading information to Commissioners, etc.

54.—(1) Any person who knowingly or recklessly provides the Commissioners with information which is false or misleading in a material particular shall be guilty of an offence if the information—

(a) is provided in purported compliance with a requirement imposed by or under a relevant enactment; or

(b) is provided otherwise than as mentioned in paragraph (a) but in circumstances in which the person providing the information intends, or could reasonably be expected to know, that it would be used by the Commissioners for the purpose of discharging their functions under a relevant enactment.

(2) Any person who wilfully alters, suppresses, conceals or destroys any document which he is or is liable to be required, by or under a relevant enactment, to produce to the Commissioners shall be guilty of an offence.

(3) Any person guilty of an offence under this section shall be liable—

(a) on summary conviction, to a fine not exceeding the statutory maximum;

(b) on conviction on indictment, to imprisonment for a term not exceeding two years or to a fine, or both.

(4) In this section—

(a) "relevant enactment" means this Act, the 1960 Act or the Charitable Trustees Incorporation Act 1872; and

1872 c.24.

(b) references to the Commissioners include references to any person conducting an inquiry under section 6 of the 1960 Act (general power to institute inquiries).

Restriction on institution of proceedings for certain offences.

55.—(1) No proceedings for an offence to which this section applies shall be instituted except by or with the consent of the Director of Public Prosecutions.

(2) This section applies to any offence under—

(a) section 3 above;

(b) section 20(10) of the 1960 Act, as amended by section 8 above;

(c) section 27 above;

(d) section 46(1) above; or

(e) section 54 above.

56.—(1) If a person fails to comply with any requirement imposed by or under—

(a) this Part of this Act,

(b) the 1960 Act, or

(c) the 1872 Act,

then (subject to subsection (2)) the Commissioners may by order give him such directions as they consider appropriate for securing that the default is made good.

(2) Subsection (1) does not apply to any such requirement if—

(a) a person who fails to comply with, or is persistently in default in relation to, the requirement is liable to any criminal penalty; or

(b) the requirement is imposed—

(i) by an order of the Commissioners to which section 41 of the 1960 Act (enforcement of orders as for contempt of High Court) applies (whether by virtue of subsection (3) below or otherwise), or

(ii) by a direction of the Commissioners to which that section applies by virtue of section 57(2) below.

(3) Section 41 of the 1960 Act applies to any order made by the Commissioners under subsection (1) above or under any of the following provisions, namely—

(a) section 12 above,

(b) section 22(2) above,

(c) section 46 above, and

(d) section 12A of the 1872 Act,

as that section applies to any such order of the Commissioners as is mentioned in that section.

(4) Subject to subsection (5) below, section 40 of the 1960 Act (miscellaneous provisions as to orders of Commissioners) shall apply to any order made by the Commissioners under this Act or the 1872 Act as it applies to any order made by them under the 1960 Act (the second reference to that Act in subsection (3) of that section being read as a reference to this Act or the 1872 Act, as the case may require).

(5) Subsection (3) of that section does not apply by virtue of subsection (4) above to any order made by the Commissioners under section 72 below or under section 12A of the 1872 Act.

(6) In this section "the 1872 Act" means the Charitable Trustees Incorporation Act 1872.

57.—(1) Any direction given by the Commissioners under any provision contained in this Part of this Act or in the 1960 Act—

(a) may be varied or revoked by a further direction given under that provision; and

(b) shall be given in writing.

PART I
Enforcement of
requirements by
order of
Commissioners,
and other
provisions as to
orders made by
them.

1872 c.24.

Directions of the
Commissioners.

PART I

(2) In the 1960 Act—

(a) subsections (1), (2) and (4) of section 40 (miscellaneous provisions as to orders of Commissioners) shall apply to any such direction as they apply to an order made by the Commissioners under that Act; and

(b) section 41 (enforcement of orders as for contempt of High Court) shall apply to any such direction as it applies to any such order of the Commissioners as is mentioned in that section.

(3) In subsection (1) the reference to the Commissioners includes, in relation to a direction under section 6(3) of the 1960 Act (general power to institute inquiries), a reference to any person conducting an inquiry under that section.

(4) Nothing in this section shall be read as applying to any directions contained in an order made by the Commissioners under section 56(1) above.

PART II

CONTROL OF FUND-RAISING FOR CHARITABLE INSTITUTIONS

Preliminary

Interpretation of Part II.

58.—(1) In this Part—

"charitable contributions", in relation to any representation made by any commercial participator or other person, means—

(a) the whole or part of—

(i) the consideration given for goods or services sold or supplied by him, or

(ii) any proceeds (other than such consideration) of a promotional venture undertaken by him, or

(b) sums given by him by way of donation in connection with the sale or supply of any such goods or services (whether the amount of such sums is determined by reference to the value of any such goods or services or otherwise);

"charitable institution" means a charity or an institution (other than a charity) which is established for charitable, benevolent or philanthropic purposes;

1960 c.58.

"charity" means a charity within the meaning of the Charities Act 1960;

"commercial participator", in relation to any charitable institution, means any person who—

(a) carries on for gain a business other than a fund-raising business, but

(b) in the course of that business, engages in any promotional venture in the course of which it is represented that charitable contributions are to be given to or applied for the benefit of the institution;

1989 c.40.

"company" has the meaning given by section 46 of the Charities Act 1960 (as amended by the Companies Act 1989);

"the court" means the High Court or a county court;

1974 c.39.

"credit card" means a card which is a credit-token within the meaning of the Consumer Credit Act 1974;

"debit card" means a card the use of which by its holder to make a payment results in a current account of his at a bank, or at any other institution providing banking services, being debited with the payment;

"fund-raising business" means any business carried on for gain and wholly or primarily engaged in soliciting or otherwise procuring money or other property for charitable, benevolent or philanthropic purposes;

"institution" includes any trust or undertaking;

"professional fund-raiser" means—

(a) any person (apart from a charitable institution) who carries on a fund-raising business, or

(b) any other person (apart from a person excluded by virtue of subsection (2) or (3)) who for reward solicits money or other property for the benefit of a charitable institution, if he does so otherwise than in the course of any fund-raising venture undertaken by a person falling within paragraph (a) above;

"promotional venture" means any advertising or sales campaign or any other venture undertaken for promotional purposes;

"radio or television programme" includes any item included in a programme service within the meaning of the Broadcasting Act 1990. 1990 c.42.

(2) In subsection (1), paragraph (b) of the definition of "professional fund-raiser" does not apply to any of the following, namely—

(a) any charitable institution or any company connected with any such institution;

(b) any officer or employee of any such institution or company, or any trustee of any such institution, acting (in each case) in his capacity as such;

(c) any person acting as a collector in respect of a public charitable collection (apart from a person who is to be treated as a promoter of such a collection by virtue of section 65(3));

(d) any person who in the course of a relevant programme, that is to say a radio or television programme in the course of which a fund-raising venture is undertaken by—

(i) a charitable institution, or

(ii) a company connected with such an institution,

makes any solicitation at the instance of that institution or company; or

(e) any commercial participator;

and for this purpose "collector" and "public charitable collection" have the same meaning as in Part III of this Act.

(3) In addition, paragraph (b) of the definition of "professional fund-raiser" does not apply to a person if he does not receive—

(a) more than—

(i) £5 per day, or

(ii) £500 per year,

by way of remuneration in connection with soliciting money or other property for the benefit of the charitable institution referred to in that paragraph; or

(b) more than £500 by way of remuneration in connection with any fund-raising venture in the course of which he solicits money or other property for the benefit of that institution.

(4) In this Part any reference to charitable purposes, where occurring in the context of a reference to charitable, benevolent or philanthropic purposes, is a reference to charitable purposes whether or not the purposes are charitable within the meaning of any rule of law.

(5) For the purposes of this Part a company is connected with a charitable institution if—

(a) the institution, or

(b) the institution and one or more other charitable institutions, taken together,

is or are entitled (whether directly or through one or more nominees) to exercise, or control the exercise of, the whole of the voting power at any general meeting of the company.

(6) In this Part—

(a) "represent" and "solicit" mean respectively represent and solicit in any manner whatever, whether expressly or impliedly and whether done—

(i) by speaking directly to the person or persons to whom the representation or solicitation is addressed (whether when in his or their presence or not), or

(ii) by means of a statement published in any newspaper, film or radio or television programme,

or otherwise, and references to a representation or solicitation shall be construed accordingly; and

(b) any reference to soliciting or otherwise procuring money or other property is a reference to soliciting or otherwise procuring money or other property whether any consideration is, or is to be, given in return for the money or other property or not.

(7) Where—

(a) any solicitation of money or other property for the benefit of a charitable institution is made in accordance with arrangements between any person and that institution, and

(b) under those arrangements that person will be responsible for receiving on behalf of the institution money or other property given in response to the solicitation,

then (if he would not be so regarded apart from this subsection) that person shall be regarded for the purposes of this Part as soliciting money or other property for the benefit of the institution.

(8) Where any fund-raising venture is undertaken by a professional fund-raiser in the course of a radio or television programme, any solicitation which is made by a person in the course of the programme at the instance of the fund-raiser shall be regarded for the purposes of this

Part as made by the fund-raiser and not by that person (and shall be so regarded whether or not the solicitation is made by that person for any reward).

(9) In this Part "services" includes facilities, and in particular—

(a) access to any premises or event;

(b) membership of any organisation;

(c) the provision of advertising space; and

(d) the provision of any financial facilities;

and references to the supply of services shall be construed accordingly.

(10) The Secretary of State may by order amend subsection (3) by substituting a different sum for any sum for the time being specified there.

Control of fund-raising

59.—(1) It shall be unlawful for a professional fund-raiser to solicit money or other property for the benefit of a charitable institution unless he does so in accordance with an agreement with the institution satisfying the prescribed requirements.

Prohibition on professional fund-raiser etc. raising funds for charitable institution without an agreement in prescribed form.

(2) It shall be unlawful for a commercial participator to represent that charitable contributions are to be given to or applied for the benefit of a charitable institution unless he does so in accordance with an agreement with the institution satisfying the prescribed requirements.

(3) Where on the application of a charitable institution the court is satisfied—

(a) that any person has contravened or is contravening subsection (1) or (2) in relation to the institution, and

(b) that, unless restrained, any such contravention is likely to continue or be repeated,

the court may grant an injunction restraining the contravention; and compliance with subsection (1) or (2) shall not be enforceable otherwise than in accordance with this subsection.

(4) Where—

(a) a charitable institution makes any agreement with a professional fund-raiser or a commercial participator by virtue of which—

(i) the professional fund-raiser is authorised to solicit money or other property for the benefit of the institution, or

(ii) the commercial participator is authorised to represent that charitable contributions are to be given to or applied for the benefit of the institution,

as the case may be, but

(b) the agreement does not satisfy the prescribed requirements in any respect,

the agreement shall not be enforceable against the institution except to such extent (if any) as may be provided by an order of the court.

(5) A professional fund-raiser or commercial participator who is a party to such an agreement as is mentioned in subsection (4)(a) shall not be entitled to receive any amount by way of remuneration or expenses in respect of anything done by him in pursuance of the agreement unless—

(a) he is so entitled under any provision of the agreement, and

(b) either—

    (i) the agreement satisfies the prescribed requirements, or

    (ii) any such provision has effect by virtue of an order of the court under subsection (4).

(6) In this section "the prescribed requirements" means such requirements as are prescribed by regulations made by virtue of section 64(2)(a).

Professional fund-raisers etc. required to indicate institutions benefiting and arrangements for remuneration.

60.—(1) Where a professional fund-raiser solicits money or other property for the benefit of one or more particular charitable institutions, the solicitation shall be accompanied by a statement clearly indicating—

(a) the name or names of the institution or institutions concerned;

(b) if there is more than one institution concerned, the proportions in which the institutions are respectively to benefit; and

(c) (in general terms) the method by which the fund-raiser's remuneration in connection with the appeal is to be determined.

(2) Where a professional fund-raiser solicits money or other property for charitable, benevolent or philanthropic purposes of any description (rather than for the benefit of one or more particular charitable institutions), the solicitation shall be accompanied by a statement clearly indicating—

(a) the fact that he is soliciting money or other property for those purposes and not for the benefit of any particular charitable institution or institutions;

(b) the method by which it is to be determined how the proceeds of the appeal are to be distributed between different charitable institutions; and

(c) (in general terms) the method by which his remuneration in connection with the appeal is to be determined.

(3) Where any representation is made by a commercial participator to the effect that charitable contributions are to be given to or applied for the benefit of one or more particular charitable institutions, the representation shall be accompanied by a statement clearly indicating—

(a) the name or names of the institution or institutions concerned;

(b) if there is more than one institution concerned, the proportions in which the institutions are respectively to benefit; and

(c) (in general terms) the method by which it is to be determined—

    (i) what proportion of the consideration given for goods or services sold or supplied by him, or of any other proceeds of a promotional venture undertaken by him, is to be given to or applied for the benefit of the institution or institutions concerned, or

    (ii) what sums by way of donations by him in connection with the sale or supply of any such goods or services are to be so given or applied,

as the case may require.

(4) If any such solicitation or representation as is mentioned in any of subsections (1) to (3) is made—

(a) in the course of a radio or television programme, and

(b) in association with an announcement to the effect that payment may be made, in response to the solicitation or representation, by means of a credit or debit card,

the statement required by virtue of subsection (1), (2) or (3) (as the case may be) shall include full details of the right to have refunded under section 61(1) any payment of £50 or more which is so made.

(5) If any such solicitation or representation as is mentioned in any of subsections (1) to (3) is made orally but is not made—

(a) by speaking directly to the particular person or persons to whom it is addressed and in his or their presence, or

(b) in the course of any radio or television programme,

the professional fund-raiser or commercial participator concerned shall, within seven days of any payment of £50 or more being made to him in response to the solicitation or representation, give to the person making the payment a written statement—

(i) of the matters specified in paragraphs (a) to (c) of that subsection; and

(ii) including full details of the right to cancel under section 61(2) an agreement made in response to the solicitation or representation, and the right to have refunded under section 61(2) or (3) any payment of £50 or more made in response thereto.

(6) In subsection (5) above the reference to the making of a payment is a reference to the making of a payment of whatever nature and by whatever means, including a payment made by means of a credit card or a debit card; and for the purposes of that subsection—

(a) where the person making any such payment makes it in person, it shall be regarded as made at the time when it is so made;

(b) where the person making any such payment sends it by post, it shall be regarded as made at the time when it is posted; and

(c) where the person making any such payment makes it by giving, by telephone or by means of any other telecommunication apparatus, authority for an account to be debited with the payment, it shall be regarded as made at the time when any such authority is given.

(7) Where any requirement of subsections (1) to (5) is not complied with in relation to any solicitation or representation, the professional fund-raiser or commercial participator concerned shall be guilty of an offence and liable on summary conviction to a fine not exceeding the fifth level on the standard scale.

(8) It shall be a defence for a person charged with any such offence to prove that he took all reasonable precautions and exercised all due diligence to avoid the commission of the offence.

(9) Where the commission by any person of an offence under subsection (7) is due to the act or default of some other person, that other person shall be guilty of the offence; and a person may be charged with and convicted of the offence by virtue of this subsection whether or not proceedings are taken against the first-mentioned person.

(10) In this section—

"the appeal", in relation to any solicitation by a professional fund-raiser, means the campaign or other fund-raising venture in the course of which the solicitation is made;

"telecommunication apparatus" has the same meaning as in the Telecommunications Act 1984.

Cancellation of payments and agreements made in response to appeals.

61.—(1) Where—

    (a) a person ("the donor"), in response to any such solicitation or representation as is mentioned in any of subsections (1) to (3) of section 60 which is made in the course of a radio or television programme, makes any payment of £50 or more to the relevant fund-raiser by means of a credit card or a debit card, but

    (b) before the end of the period of seven days beginning with the date of the solicitation or representation, the donor serves on the relevant fund-raiser a notice in writing which, however expressed, indicates the donor's intention to cancel the payment,

the donor shall (subject to subsection (4) below) be entitled to have the payment refunded to him forthwith by the relevant fund-raiser.

(2) Where—

    (a) a person ("the donor"), in response to any solicitation or representation falling within subsection (5) of section 60, enters into an agreement with the relevant fund-raiser under which the donor is, or may be, liable to make any payment or payments to the relevant fund-raiser, and the amount or aggregate amount which the donor is, or may be, liable to pay to him under the agreement is £50 or more, but

    (b) before the end of the period of seven days beginning with the date when he is given any such written statement as is referred to in that subsection, the donor serves on the relevant fund-raiser a notice in writing which, however expressed, indicates the donor's intention to cancel the agreement,

the notice shall operate, as from the time when it is so served, to cancel the agreement and any liability of any person other than the donor in connection with the making of any such payment or payments, and the donor shall (subject to subsection (4) below) be entitled to have any payment of £50 or more made by him under the agreement refunded to him forthwith by the relevant fund-raiser.

(3) Where, in response to any solicitation or representation falling within subsection (5) of section 60, a person ("the donor")—

    (a) makes any payment of £50 or more to the relevant fund-raiser, but

(b) does not enter into any such agreement as is mentioned in subsection (2) above,

then, if before the end of the period of seven days beginning with the date when the donor is given any such written statement as is referred to in subsection (5) of that section, the donor serves on the relevant fund-raiser a notice in writing which, however expressed, indicates the donor's intention to cancel the payment, the donor shall (subject to subsection (4) below) be entitled to have the payment refunded to him forthwith by the relevant fund-raiser.

(4) The right of any person to have a payment refunded to him under any of subsections (1) to (3) above—

(a) is a right to have refunded to him the amount of the payment less any administrative expenses reasonably incurred by the relevant fund-raiser in connection with—

(i) the making of the refund, or

(ii) (in the case of a refund under subsection (2)) dealing with the notice of cancellation served by that person; and

(b) shall, in the case of a payment for goods already received, be conditional upon restitution being made by him of the goods in question.

(5) Nothing in subsections (1) to (3) above has effect in relation to any payment made or to be made in respect of services which have been supplied at the time when the relevant notice is served.

(6) In this section any reference to the making of a payment is a reference to the making of a payment of whatever nature and (in the case of subsection (2) or (3)) a payment made by whatever means, including a payment made by means of a credit card or a debit card; and subsection (6) of section 60 shall have effect for determining when a payment is made for the purposes of this section as it has effect for determining when a payment is made for the purposes of subsection (5) of that section.

(7) In this section "the relevant fund-raiser", in relation to any solicitation or representation, means the professional fund-raiser or commercial participator by whom it is made.

(8) The Secretary of State may by order—

(a) amend any provision of this section by substituting a different sum for the sum for the time being specified there; and

(b) make such consequential amendments in section 60 as he considers appropriate.

62.—(1) Where on the application of any charitable institution—

(a) the court is satisfied that any person has done or is doing either of the following, namely—

(i) soliciting money or other property for the benefit of the institution, or

(ii) representing that charitable contributions are to be given to or applied for the benefit of the institution,

and that, unless restrained, he is likely to do further acts of that nature, and

Right of charitable institution to prevent unauthorised fund-raising.

(b) the court is also satisfied as to one or more of the matters specified in subsection (2),

then (subject to subsection (3)) the court may grant an injunction restraining the doing of any such acts.

(2) The matters referred to in subsection (1)(b) are—

(a) that the person in question is using methods of fund-raising to which the institution objects;

(b) that that person is not a fit and proper person to raise funds for the institution; and

(c) where the conduct complained of is the making of such representations as are mentioned in subsection (1)(a)(ii), that the institution does not wish to be associated with the particular promotional or other fund-raising venture in which that person is engaged.

(3) The power to grant an injunction under subsection (1) shall not be exercisable on the application of a charitable institution unless the institution has, not less than 28 days before making the application, served on the person in question a notice in writing—

(a) requesting him to cease forthwith—

(i) soliciting money or other property for the benefit of the institution, or

(ii) representing that charitable contributions are to be given to or applied for the benefit of the institution,

as the case may be; and

(b) stating that, if he does not comply with the notice, the institution will make an application under this section for an injunction.

(4) Where—

(a) a charitable institution has served on any person a notice under subsection (3) ("the relevant notice") and that person has complied with the notice, but

(b) that person has subsequently begun to carry on activities which are the same, or substantially the same, as those in respect of which the relevant notice was served,

the institution shall not, in connection with an application made by it under this section in respect of the activities carried on by that person, be required by virtue of that subsection to serve a further notice on him, if the application is made not more than 12 months after the date of service of the relevant notice.

(5) This section shall not have the effect of authorising a charitable institution to make an application under this section in respect of anything done by a professional fund-raiser or commercial participator in relation to the institution.

False statements relating to institutions which are not registered charities.

63.—(1) Where—

(a) a person solicits money or other property for the benefit of an institution in association with a representation that the institution is a registered charity, and

(b) the institution is not such a charity,

he shall be guilty of an offence and liable on summary conviction to a fine not exceeding the fifth level on the standard scale.

(2) In subsection (1) "registered charity" means a charity which is for the time being registered in the register of charities kept under section 4 of the Charities Act 1960.

1960 c.58.

Supplementary

64.—(1) The Secretary of State may make such regulations as appear to him to be necessary or desirable for any purposes connected with any of the preceding provisions of this Part.

Regulations about fund-raising.

(2) Without prejudice to the generality of subsection (1), any such regulations may—

(a) prescribe the form and content of—

(i) agreements made for the purposes of section 59, and

(ii) notices served under section 62(3);

(b) require professional fund-raisers or commercial participators who are parties to such agreements with charitable institutions to make available to the institutions books, documents or other records (however kept) which relate to the institutions;

(c) specify the manner in which money or other property acquired by professional fund-raisers or commercial participators for the benefit of, or otherwise falling to be given to or applied by such persons for the benefit of, charitable institutions is to be transmitted to such institutions;

(d) provide for any provisions of section 60 or 61 having effect in relation to solicitations or representations made in the course of radio or television programmes to have effect, subject to any modifications specified in the regulations, in relation to solicitations or representations made in the course of such programmes—

(i) by charitable institutions, or

(ii) by companies connected with such institutions,

and, in that connection, provide for any other provisions of this Part to have effect for the purposes of the regulations subject to any modifications so specified;

(e) make other provision regulating the raising of funds for charitable, benevolent or philanthropic purposes (whether by professional fund-raisers or commercial participators or otherwise).

(3) In subsection (2)(c) the reference to such money or other property as is there mentioned includes a reference to money or other property which, in the case of a professional fund-raiser or commercial participator—

(a) has been acquired by him otherwise than in accordance with an agreement with a charitable institution, but

(b) by reason of any solicitation or representation in consequence of which it has been acquired, is held by him on trust for such an institution.

(4) Regulations under this section may provide that any failure to comply with a specified provision of the regulations shall be an offence punishable on summary conviction by a fine not exceeding the second level on the standard scale.

PART III

PUBLIC CHARITABLE COLLECTIONS

Preliminary

Interpretation of Part III.

65.—(1) In this Part—

(a) "public charitable collection" means (subject to subsection (2)) a charitable appeal which is made—

    (i) in any public place, or

    (ii) by means of visits from house to house; and

(b) "charitable appeal" means an appeal to members of the public to give money or other property (whether for consideration or otherwise) which is made in association with a representation that the whole or any part of its proceeds is to be applied for charitable, benevolent or philanthropic purposes.

(2) Subsection (1)(a) does not apply to a charitable appeal which—

(a) is made in the course of a public meeting; or

(b) is made—

    (i) on land within a churchyard or burial ground contiguous or adjacent to a place of public worship, or

    (ii) on other land occupied for the purposes of a place of public worship and contiguous or adjacent to it,

being (in each case) land which is enclosed or substantially enclosed (whether by any wall or building or otherwise); or

(c) is an appeal to members of the public to give money or other property by placing it in an unattended receptacle;

and for the purposes of paragraph (c) above a receptacle is unattended if it is not in the possession or custody of a person acting as a collector.

(3) In this Part, in relation to a public charitable collection—

(a) "promoter" means a person who (whether alone or with others and whether for remuneration or otherwise) organises or controls the conduct of the charitable appeal in question, and associated expressions shall be construed accordingly; and

(b) "collector" means any person by whom that appeal is made (whether made by him alone or with others and whether made by him for remuneration or otherwise);

but where no person acts in the manner mentioned in paragraph (a) above in respect of a public charitable collection, any person who acts as a collector in respect of it shall for the purposes of this Part be treated as a promoter of it as well.

(4) In this Part—

"local authority" means the council of a district or of a London borough, the Common Council of the City of London, or the Council of the Isles of Scilly; and "proceeds", in relation to a public charitable collection, means all money or other property given (whether for consideration or otherwise) in response to the charitable appeal in question.

(5) In this Part any reference to charitable purposes, where occurring in the context of a reference to charitable, benevolent or philanthropic purposes, is a reference to charitable purposes whether or not the purposes are charitable within the meaning of any rule of law.

(6) The functions exercisable under this Part by a local authority shall be exercisable—

(a) as respects the Inner Temple, by its Sub-Treasurer, and

(b) as respects the Middle Temple, by its Under Treasurer;

and references in this Part to a local authority or to the area of a local authority shall be construed accordingly.

(7) It is hereby declared that an appeal to members of the public (other than one falling within subsection (2)) is a public charitable collection for the purposes of this Part if—

(a) it consists in or includes the making of an offer to sell goods or to supply services, or the exposing of goods for sale, to members of the public, and

(b) it is made as mentioned in sub-paragraph (i) or (ii) of subsection (1)(a) and in association with a representation that the whole or any part of its proceeds is to be applied for charitable, benevolent or philanthropic purposes.

This subsection shall not be taken as prejudicing the generality of subsection (1)(b).

(8) In this section—

"house" includes any part of a building constituting a separate dwelling;

"public place", in relation to a charitable appeal, means—

(a) any highway, and

(b) (subject to subsection (9)) any other place to which, at any time when the appeal is made, members of the public have or are permitted to have access and which either—

(i) is not within a building, or

(ii) if within a building, is a public area within any station, airport or shopping precinct or any other similar public area.

(9) In subsection (8), paragraph (b) of the definition of "public place" does not apply to—

(a) any place to which members of the public are permitted to have access only if any payment or ticket required as a condition of access has been made or purchased; or

(b) any place to which members of the public are permitted to have access only by virtue of permission given for the purposes of the appeal in question.

Prohibition on conducting unauthorised collections

Prohibition on conducting public charitable collections without authorisation.

66.—(1) No public charitable collection shall be conducted in the area of any local authority except in accordance with—

(a) a permit issued by the authority under section 68; or

(b) an order made by the Charity Commissioners under section 72.

(2) Where a public charitable collection is conducted in contravention of subsection (1), any promoter of that collection shall be guilty of an offence and liable on summary conviction to a fine not exceeding the fourth level on the standard scale.

Permits

Applications for permits to conduct public charitable collections.

67.—(1) An application for a permit to conduct a public charitable collection in the area of a local authority shall be made to the authority by the person or persons proposing to promote that collection.

(2) Any such application—

(a) shall specify the period for which it is desired that the permit, if issued, should have effect, being a period not exceeding 12 months; and

(b) shall contain such information as may be prescribed by regulations under section 73.

(3) Any such application—

(a) shall be made at least one month before the relevant day or before such later date as the local authority may in the case of that application allow, but

(b) shall not be made more than six months before the relevant day;

and for this purpose "the relevant day" means the day on which the collection is to be conducted or, where it is to be conducted on more than one day, the first of those days.

(4) Before determining any application duly made to them under this section, a local authority shall consult the chief officer of police for the police area which comprises or includes their area and may make such other inquiries as they think fit.

Determination of applications and issue of permits.

68.—(1) Where an application for a permit is duly made to a local authority under section 67 in respect of a public charitable collection, the authority shall either—

(a) issue a permit in respect of the collection, or

(b) refuse the application on one or more of the grounds specified in section 69,

and, where they issue such a permit, it shall (subject to section 70) have effect for the period specified in the application in accordance with section 67(2)(a).

(2) A local authority may, at the time of issuing a permit under this section, attach to it such conditions as they think fit, having regard to the local circumstances of the collection; but the authority shall secure that the terms of any such conditions are consistent with the provisions of any regulations under section 73.

(3) Without prejudice to the generality of subsection (2), a local authority may attach conditions—

  (a) specifying the day of the week, date, time or frequency of the collection;

  (b) specifying the locality or localities within their area in which the collection may be conducted;

  (c) regulating the manner in which the collection is to be conducted.

(4) Where a local authority—

  (a) refuse to issue a permit, or

  (b) attach any condition to a permit under subsection (2),

they shall serve on the applicant written notice of their decision to do so and of the reasons for their decision; and that notice shall also state the right of appeal conferred by section 71(1) or (as the case may be) section 71(2), and the time within which such an appeal must be brought.

69.—(1) A local authority may refuse to issue a permit to conduct a public charitable collection on any of the following grounds, namely—

  (a) that it appears to them that the collection would cause undue inconvenience to members of the public by reason of—

      (i) the day of the week or date on which,

      (ii) the time at which,

      (iii) the frequency with which, or

      (iv) the locality or localities in which,

    it is proposed to be conducted;

  (b) that the collection is proposed to be conducted on a day on which another public charitable collection is already authorised (whether under section 68 or otherwise) to be conducted in the authority's area, or on the day falling immediately before, or immediately after, any such day;

  (c) that it appears to them that the amount likely to be applied for charitable, benevolent or philanthropic purposes in consequence of the collection would be inadequate, having regard to the likely amount of the proceeds of the collection;

  (d) that it appears to them that the applicant or any other person would be likely to receive an excessive amount by way of remuneration in connection with the collection;

  (e) that the applicant has been convicted—

      (i) of an offence under section 5 of the 1916 Act, under the 1939 Act, under section 119 of the 1982 Act or regulations made under it, or under this Part or regulations made under section 73 below, or

      (ii) of any offence involving dishonesty or of a kind the commission of which would in their opinion be likely to be facilitated by the issuing to him of a permit under section 68 above;

  (f) where the applicant is a person other than a charitable, benevolent or philanthropic institution for whose benefit the collection is proposed to be conducted, that they are not satisfied that the applicant is authorised (whether by any such institution or by any person acting on behalf of any such institution) to promote the collection; or

(g) that it appears to them that the applicant, in promoting any other collection authorised under this Part or under section 119 of the 1982 Act, failed to exercise due diligence—

(i) to secure that persons authorised by him to act as collectors for the purposes of the collection were fit and proper persons;

(ii) to secure that such persons complied with the provisions of regulations under section 73 below or (as the case may be) section 119 of the 1982 Act; or

(iii) to prevent badges or certificates of authority being obtained by persons other than those he had so authorised.

(2) A local authority shall not, however, refuse to issue such a permit on the ground mentioned in subsection (1)(b) if it appears to them—

(a) that the collection would be conducted only in one location, which is on land to which members of the public would have access only by virtue of the express or implied permission of the occupier of the land; and

(b) that the occupier of the land consents to the collection being conducted there;

and for this purpose "the occupier", in relation to unoccupied land, means the person entitled to occupy it.

(3) In subsection (1)—

(a) in the case of a collection in relation to which there is more than one applicant, any reference to the applicant shall be construed as a reference to any of the applicants; and

(b) (subject to subsection (4)) the reference in paragraph (g)(iii) to badges or certificates of authority is a reference to badges or certificates of authority in a form prescribed by regulations under section 73 below or (as the case may be) under section 119 of the 1982 Act.

(4) Subsection (1)(g) applies to the conduct of the applicant (or any of the applicants) in relation to any public charitable collection authorised under regulations made under section 5 of the 1916 Act (collection of money or sale of articles in a street or other public place), or authorised under the 1939 Act (collection of money or other property by means of visits from house to house), as it applies to his conduct in relation to a collection authorised under this Part, subject to the following modifications, namely—

(a) in the case of a collection authorised under regulations made under the 1916 Act—

(i) the reference in sub-paragraph (ii) to regulations under section 73 below shall be construed as a reference to the regulations under which the collection in question was authorised, and

(ii) the reference in sub-paragraph (iii) to badges or certificates of authority shall be construed as a reference to any written authority provided to a collector pursuant to those regulations; and

(b) in the case of a collection authorised under the 1939 Act—

    (i) the reference in sub-paragraph (ii) to regulations under section 73 below shall be construed as a reference to regulations under section 4 of that Act, and

    (ii) the reference in sub-paragraph (iii) to badges or certificates of authority shall be construed as a reference to badges or certificates of authority in a form prescribed by such regulations.

(5) In this section—

"the 1916 Act" means the Police, Factories, &c. (Miscellaneous Provisions) Act 1916; 1916 c.31.

"the 1939 Act" means the House to House Collections Act 1939; and 1939 c.44.

"the 1982 Act" means the Civic Government (Scotland) Act 1982. 1982 c.45.

70.—(1) Where a local authority who have issued a permit under section 68— Withdrawal etc. of permits.

(a) have reason to believe that there has been a change in the circumstances which prevailed at the time when they issued the permit, and are of the opinion that, if the application for the permit had been made in the new circumstances of the case, the permit would not have been issued by them, or

(b) have reason to believe that any information furnished to them by the promoter (or, in the case of a collection in relation to which there is more than one promoter, by any of them) for the purposes of the application for the permit was false in a material particular,

then (subject to subsection (2)) they may—

(i) withdraw the permit;

(ii) attach any condition to the permit; or

(iii) vary any existing condition of the permit.

(2) Any condition imposed by the local authority under subsection (1) (whether by attaching a new condition to the permit or by varying an existing condition) must be one that could have been attached to the permit under section 68(2) at the time when it was issued, assuming for this purpose—

(a) that the new circumstances of the case had prevailed at that time, or

(b) (in a case falling within paragraph (b) of subsection (1) above) that the authority had been aware of the true circumstances of the case at that time.

(3) Where a local authority who have issued a permit under section 68 have reason to believe that there has been or is likely to be a breach of any condition of it, or that a breach of such a condition is continuing, they may withdraw the permit.

(4) Where under this section a local authority withdraw, attach any condition to, or vary an existing condition of, a permit, they shall serve on the promoter written notice of their decision to do so and of the reasons for their decision; and that notice shall also state the right of appeal conferred by section 71(2) and the time within which such an appeal must be brought.

(5) Where a local authority so withdraw, attach any condition to, or vary an existing condition of, a permit, the permit shall nevertheless continue to have effect as if it had not been withdrawn or (as the case may be) as if the condition had not been attached or the variation had not been made—

    (a) until the time for bringing an appeal under section 71(2) has expired, or

    (b) if such an appeal is duly brought, until the determination or abandonment of the appeal.

Appeals.

71.—(1) A person who has duly applied to a local authority under section 67 for a permit to conduct a public charitable collection in the authority's area may appeal to a magistrates' court against a decision of the authority to refuse to issue a permit to him.

(2) A person to whom a permit has been issued under section 68 may appeal to a magistrates' court against—

    (a) a decision of the local authority under that section or section 70 to attach any condition to the permit; or

    (b) a decision of the local authority under section 70 to vary any condition so attached or to withdraw the permit.

1980 c.43.

(3) An appeal under subsection (1) or (2) shall be by way of complaint for an order, and the Magistrates' Courts Act 1980 shall apply to the proceedings; and references in this section to a magistrates' court are to a magistrates' court acting for the petty sessions area in which is situated the office or principal office of the local authority against whose decision the appeal is brought.

(4) Any such appeal shall be brought within 14 days of the date of service on the person in question of the relevant notice under section 68(4) or (as the case may be) section 70(4); and for the purposes of this subsection an appeal shall be taken to be brought when the complaint is made.

(5) An appeal against the decision of a magistrates' court on an appeal under subsection (1) or (2) may be brought to the Crown Court.

(6) On an appeal to a magistrates' court or the Crown Court under this section, the court may confirm, vary or reverse the local authority's decision and generally give such directions as it thinks fit, having regard to the provisions of this Part and of regulations under section 73.

(7) It shall be the duty of the local authority to comply with any directions given by the court under subsection (6); but the authority need not comply with any directions given by a magistrates' court—

    (a) until the time for bringing an appeal under subsection (5) has expired, or

    (b) if such an appeal is duly brought, until the determination or abandonment of the appeal.

Orders made by Charity Commissioners

72.—(1) Where the Charity Commissioners are satisfied, on the application of any charity, that that charity proposes—

    (a) to promote public charitable collections—

        (i) throughout England and Wales, or

        (ii) throughout a substantial part of England and Wales,

    in connection with any charitable purposes pursued by the charity, or

    (b) to authorise other persons to promote public charitable collections as mentioned in paragraph (a),

the Commissioners may make an order under this subsection in respect of the charity.

(2) Such an order shall have the effect of authorising public charitable collections which—

    (a) are promoted by the charity in respect of which the order is made, or by persons authorised by the charity, and

    (b) are so promoted in connection with the charitable purposes mentioned in subsection (1),

to be conducted in such area or areas as may be specified in the order.

(3) An order under subsection (1) may—

    (a) include such conditions as the Commissioners think fit;

    (b) be expressed (without prejudice to paragraph (c)) to have effect without limit of time, or for a specified period only;

    (c) be revoked or varied by a further order of the Commissioners.

(4) Where the Commissioners, having made an order under subsection (1) in respect of a charity, make any further order revoking or varying that order, they shall serve on the charity written notice of their reasons for making the further order, unless it appears to them that the interests of the charity would not be prejudiced by the further order.

(5) In this section "charity" and "charitable purposes" have the same meaning as in the Charities Act 1960.

Supplementary

73.—(1) The Secretary of State may make regulations—

    (a) prescribing the information which is to be contained in applications made under section 67;

    (b) for the purpose of regulating the conduct of public charitable collections authorised under—

        (i) permits issued under section 68; or

        (ii) orders made by the Charity Commissioners under section 72.

(2) Regulations under subsection (1)(b) may, without prejudice to the generality of that provision, make provision—

    (a) about the keeping and publication of accounts;

    (b) for the prevention of annoyance to members of the public;

(c) with respect to the use by collectors of badges and certificates of authority, or badges incorporating such certificates, and to other matters relating to such badges and certificates, including, in particular, provision—

(i) prescribing the form of such badges and certificates;

(ii) requiring a collector, on request, to permit his badge, or any certificate of authority held by him for the purposes of the collection, to be inspected by a constable or a duly authorised officer of a local authority, or by an occupier of any premises visited by him in the course of the collection;

(d) for prohibiting persons under a prescribed age from acting as collectors, and prohibiting others from causing them so to act.

(3) Regulations under this section may provide that any failure to comply with a specified provision of the regulations shall be an offence punishable on summary conviction by a fine not exceeding the second level on the standard scale.

Offences.

74.—(1) A person shall be guilty of an offence if, in connection with any charitable appeal, he displays or uses—

(a) a prescribed badge or a prescribed certificate of authority which is not for the time being held by him for the purposes of the appeal pursuant to regulations under section 73, or

(b) any badge or article, or any certificate or other document, so nearly resembling a prescribed badge or (as the case may be) a prescribed certificate of authority as to be likely to deceive a member of the public.

(2) A person guilty of an offence under subsection (1) shall be liable on summary conviction to a fine not exceeding the fourth level on the standard scale.

(3) Any person who, for the purposes of an application made under section 67, knowingly or recklessly furnishes any information which is false in a material particular shall be guilty of an offence and liable on summary conviction to a fine not exceeding the fourth level on the standard scale.

(4) In subsection (1) "prescribed badge" and "prescribed certificate of authority" mean respectively a badge and a certificate of authority in such form as may be prescribed by regulations under section 73.

PART IV

GENERAL

Offences by bodies corporate.

1960 c.58.

75. Where any offence—

(a) under this Act or any regulations made under it, or

(b) under the Charities Act 1960,

is committed by a body corporate and is proved to have been committed with the consent or connivance of, or to be attributable to any neglect on the part of, any director, manager, secretary or other similar officer of the body corporate, or any person who was purporting to act in any such capacity, he as well as the body corporate shall be guilty of that offence and shall be liable to be proceeded against and punished accordingly.

In relation to a body corporate whose affairs are managed by its members, "director" means a member of the body corporate.

76.—(1) This section applies to—

   (a) any order or direction made or given by the Charity Commissioners under Part I of this Act;

   (b) any notice or other document required or authorised to be given or served under Part II of this Act; and

   (c) any notice required to be served under Part III of this Act.

(2) A document to which this section applies may be served on or given to a person (other than a body corporate)—

   (a) by delivering it to that person;

   (b) by leaving it at his last known address in the United Kingdom; or

   (c) by sending it by post to him at that address.

(3) A document to which this section applies may be served on or given to a body corporate by delivering it or sending it by post—

   (a) to the registered or principal office of the body in the United Kingdom, or

   (b) if it has no such office in the United Kingdom, to any place in the United Kingdom where it carries on business or conducts its activities (as the case may be).

(4) Any such document may also be served on or given to a person (including a body corporate) by sending it by post to that person at an address notified by that person for the purposes of this subsection to the person or persons by whom it is required or authorised to be served or given.

77.—(1) Any regulations or order of the Secretary of State under this Act—

   (a) shall be made by statutory instrument; and

   (b) (subject to subsection (2)) shall be subject to annulment in pursuance of a resolution of either House of Parliament.

(2) Subsection (1)(b) does not apply—

   (a) to an order under section 38;

   (b) to any regulations under section 39;

   (c) to a statutory instrument to which section 51(3) applies; or

   (d) to an order under section 79(2).

(3) Any regulations or order of the Secretary of State under this Act may make—

   (a) different provision for different cases; and

   (b) such supplemental, incidental, consequential or transitional provision or savings as the Secretary of State considers appropriate.

(4) Before making any regulations under section 20, 22, 23, 64 or 73 the Secretary of State shall consult such persons or bodies of persons as he considers appropriate.

78.—(1) The enactments mentioned in Schedule 6 to this Act shall have effect subject to the amendments there specified (which are either minor amendments or amendments consequential on the provisions of this Act).

(2) The enactments mentioned in Schedule 7 to this Act (which include some that are already spent or are no longer of practical utility) are hereby repealed to the extent specified in the third column of that Schedule.

79.—(1) This Act may be cited as the Charities Act 1992.

(2) This Act shall come into force on such day as the Secretary of State may by order appoint; and different days may be so appointed for different provisions or for different purposes.

(3) Subject to subsections (4) to (6) below, this Act extends only to England and Wales.

(4) Section 52 and this section extend to the whole of the United Kingdom.

(5) Sections 38 and 39, and so much of section 77 as relates to those sections, extend to England and Wales and Scotland.

(6) The amendments in Schedule 6, and (subject to subsection (7)) the repeals in Schedule 7, have the same extent as the enactments to which they refer, and section 78 extends accordingly.

(7) The repeal in Schedule 7 of the Police, Factories, &c. (Miscellaneous Provisions) Act 1916 does not extend to Northern Ireland.

SCHEDULES

SCHEDULE 1

SECTIONS 4 AND 20 OF THE CHARITIES ACT 1960, AS AMENDED

Section 4

4.—(1) The Commissioners shall continue to keep a register of charities, which shall be kept by them in such manner as they think fit.

The register of charities.

(2) There shall be entered in the register every charity not excepted by subsection (4) below; and a charity so excepted (other than one excepted by paragraph (a) of that subsection) may be entered in the register at the request of the charity, but (whether or not it was excepted at the time of registration) may at any time, and shall at the request of the charity, be removed from the register.

(2A) The register shall contain—

(a) the name of every registered charity; and

(b) such other particulars of, and such other information relating to, every such charity as the Commissioners think fit.

(3) Any institution which no longer appears to the Commissioners to be a charity shall be removed from the register, with effect, where the removal is due to any change in its purposes or trusts, from the date of that change; and there shall also be removed from the register any charity which ceases to exist or does not operate.

(4) The following charities are not required to be registered, that is to say,—

(a) any charity comprised in the Second Schedule to this Act (in this Act referred to as an "exempt charity");

(b) any charity which is excepted by order or regulations;

(c) any charity which has neither—

(i) any permanent endowment, nor

(ii) the use or occupation of any land,

and whose income from all sources does not in aggregate amount to more than £1,000 a year;

and no charity is required to be registered in respect of any registered place of worship.

(5) With any application for a charity to be registered there shall be supplied to the Commissioners copies of its trusts (or, if they are not set out in any extant document, particulars of them), and such other documents or information as may be prescribed or as the Commissioners may require for the purpose of the application.

(6) It shall be the duty—

(a) of the charity trustees of any charity which is not registered nor excepted from registration to apply for it to be registered, and to supply the documents and information required by subsection (5) above; and

(b) of the charity trustees (or last charity trustees) of any institution which is for the time being registered to notify the Commissioners if it ceases to exist, or if there is any change in its trusts, or in the particulars of it entered in the register, and to supply to the Commissioners particulars of any such change and copies of any new trusts or alterations of the trusts.

(7) The register (including the entries cancelled when institutions are removed from the register) shall be open to public inspection at all reasonable times; and copies (or particulars) of the trusts of any registered charity as supplied to the Commissioners under this section shall, so long as it remains on the register, be kept by them and be open to public inspection at all reasonable times, except in so far as regulations otherwise provide.

(7A) Where any information contained in the register is not in documentary form, subsection (7) above shall be construed as requiring the information to be available for public inspection in legible form at all reasonable times.

(7B) If the Commissioners so determine, that subsection shall not apply to any particular information contained in the register and specified in their determination.

(8) Nothing in the foregoing subsections shall require any person to supply the Commissioners with copies of schemes for the administration of a charity made otherwise than by the court, or to notify the Commissioners of any change made with respect to a registered charity by such a scheme, or require a person, if he refers the Commissioners to a document or copy already in the possession of the Commissioners, to supply a further copy of the document; but where by virtue of this subsection a copy of any document need not be supplied to the Commissioners, a copy of it, if it relates to a registered charity, shall be open to inspection under subsection (7) above as if supplied to the Commissioners under this section.

(8A) If he thinks it expedient to do so—

    (a) in consequence of changes in the value of money, or

    (b) with a view to extending the scope of the exception provided for by subsection (4)(c) above,

the Secretary of State may by order amend subsection (4)(c) by substituting a different sum for the sum for the time being specified there.

(8B) Any such order shall be made by statutory instrument subject to annulment in pursuance of a resolution of either House of Parliament.

(9) In this section "registered place of worship" means any land or building falling within section nine of the Places of Worship Registration Act, 1855, as amended by this Act (that is to say, the land and buildings which, if this Act had not been passed, would by virtue of that section as amended by subsequent enactments be partially exempted from the operation of the Charitable Trusts Act, 1853), and for the purposes of this subsection "building" includes part of a building.

Section 20

Power to act for protection of charities.

20.—(1) Where, at any time after they have instituted an inquiry under section 6 of this Act with respect to any charity, the Commissioners are satisfied—

    (a) that there is or has been any misconduct or mismanagement in the administration of the charity; or

    (b) that it is necessary or desirable to act for the purpose of protecting the property of the charity or securing a proper application for the purposes of the charity of that property or of property coming to the charity;

the Commissioners may of their own motion do one or more of the following things, namely—

    (i) by order suspend any trustee, charity trustee, officer, agent or employee of the charity from the exercise of his office or employment pending consideration being given to his removal (whether under this section or otherwise);

(ii) by order appoint such number of additional charity trustees as they consider necessary for the proper administration of the charity;

(iii) by order vest any property held by or in trust for the charity in the official custodian for charities, or require the persons in whom any such property is vested to transfer it to him, or appoint any person to transfer any such property to him;

(iv) order any person who holds any property on behalf of the charity, or of any trustee for it, not to part with the property without the approval of the Commissioners;

(v) order any debtor of the charity not to make any payment in or towards the discharge of his liability to the charity without the approval of the Commissioners;

(vi) by order restrict (notwithstanding anything in the trusts of the charity) the transactions which may be entered into, or the nature or amount of the payments which may be made, in the administration of the charity without the approval of the Commissioners;

(vii) by order appoint (in accordance with section 20A of this Act) a receiver and manager in respect of the property and affairs of the charity.

(1A) Where, at any time after they have instituted an inquiry under section 6 of this Act with respect to any charity, the Commissioners are satisfied—

(a) that there is or has been any misconduct or mismanagement in the administration of the charity; and

(b) that it is necessary or desirable to act for the purpose of protecting the property of the charity or securing a proper application for the purposes of the charity of that property or of property coming to the charity;

the Commissioners may of their own motion do either or both of the following things, namely—

(i) by order remove any trustee, charity trustee, officer, agent or employee of the charity who has been responsible for or privy to the misconduct or mismanagement or has by his conduct contributed to it or facilitated it;

(ii) by order establish a scheme for the administration of the charity.

(2) The references in subsection (1) or (1A) above to misconduct or mismanagement shall (notwithstanding anything in the trusts of the charity) extend to the employment for the remuneration or reward of persons acting in the affairs of the charity, or for other administrative purposes, of sums which are excessive in relation to the property which is or is likely to be applied or applicable for the purposes of the charity.

(3) The Commissioners may also remove a charity trustee by order made of their own motion—

(a) where, within the last five years, the trustee—

(i) having previously been adjudged bankrupt or had his estate sequestrated, has been discharged, or

(ii) having previously made a composition or arrangement with, or granted a trust deed for, his creditors, has been discharged in respect of it;

(aa) where the trustee is a corporation in liquidation;

(ab) where the trustee is incapable of acting by reason of mental disorder within the meaning of the Mental Health Act 1983;

(b) where the trustee has not acted, and will not declare his willingness or unwillingness to act;

    (c) where the trustee is outside England and Wales or cannot be found or does not act, and his absence or failure to act impedes the proper administration of the charity.

(4) The Commissioners may by order made of their own motion appoint a person to be a charity trustee—

    (a) in place of a charity trustee removed by them under this section or otherwise;

    (b) where there are no charity trustees, or where by reason of vacancies in their number or the absence or incapacity of any of their number the charity cannot apply for the appointment;

    (c) where there is a single charity trustee, not being a corporation aggregate, and the Commissioners are of opinion that it is necessary to increase the number for the proper administration of the charity;

    (d) where the Commissioners are of opinion that it is necessary for the proper administration of the charity to have an additional charity trustee, because one of the existing charity trustees who ought nevertheless to remain a charity trustee either cannot be found or does not act or is outside England and Wales.

(5) The powers of the Commissioners under this section to remove or appoint charity trustees of their own motion shall include power to make any such order with respect to the vesting in or transfer to the charity trustees of any property as the Commissioners could make on the removal or appointment of a charity trustee by them under section eighteen of this Act.

(6) Any order under this section for the removal or appointment of a charity trustee or trustee for a charity, or for the vesting or transfer of any property, shall be of the like effect as an order made under section eighteen of this Act.

(7) Subject to subsection (7A) below, subsections (10) and (11) of section 18 of this Act shall apply to orders under this section as they apply to orders under that section.

(7A) The requirement to obtain any such certificate or leave as is mentioned in the proviso to section 18(11) shall not apply to—

    (a) an appeal by a charity or any of the charity trustees of a charity against an order under subsection (1)(vii) above appointing a receiver and manager in respect of the charity's property and affairs, or

    (b) an appeal by a person against an order under subsection (1A)(i) or (3)(a) above removing him from his office or employment.

(7B) Subsection (12) of section 18 of this Act shall apply to an order under this section which establishes a scheme for the administration of a charity as it applies to such an order under that section.

(8) The power of the Commissioners to make an order under subsection (1)(i) above shall not be exercisable so as to suspend any person from the exercise of his office or employment for a period of more than twelve months; but (without prejudice to the generality of section 40(1) of this Act) any such order made in the case of any person may make provision as respects the period of his suspension for matters arising out of it, and in particular for enabling any person to execute any instrument in his name or otherwise act for him and, in the case of a charity trustee, for adjusting any rules governing the proceedings of the charity trustees to take account of the reduction in the number capable of acting.

(9) Before exercising any jurisdiction under this section otherwise than by virtue of subsection (1) above, the Commissioners shall give notice of their intention to do so to each of the charity trustees, except any that cannot be found or has no known address in the United Kingdom; and any such notice may be given by post and, if given by post, may be addressed to the recipient's last known address in the United Kingdom.

(9A) The Commissioners shall, at such intervals as they think fit, review any order made by them under paragraph (i), or any of paragraphs (iii) to (vii), of subsection (1) above; and, if on any such review it appears to them that it would be appropriate to discharge the order in whole or in part, they shall so discharge it (whether subject to any savings or other transitional provisions or not).

(10) If any person contravenes an order under subsection (1)(iv), (v) or (vi) above, he shall be guilty of an offence and liable on summary conviction to a fine not exceeding the fifth level on the standard scale.

(10A) Subsection (10) above shall not be taken to preclude the bringing of proceedings for breach of trust against any charity trustee or trustee for a charity in respect of a contravention of an order under subsection (1)(iv) or (vi) above (whether proceedings in respect of the contravention are brought against him under subsection (10) above or not).

(12) This section shall not apply to an exempt charity.

SCHEDULE 2

MEANING OF "CONNECTED PERSON" FOR PURPOSES OF SECTION 32(2)

1. In section 32(2) "connected person", in relation to a charity, means—

(a) a charity trustee or trustee for the charity;

(b) a person who is the donor of any land to the charity (whether the gift was made on or after the establishment of the charity);

(c) a child, parent, grandchild, grandparent, brother or sister of any such trustee or donor;

(d) an officer, agent or employee of the charity;

(e) the spouse of any person falling within any of sub-paragraphs (a) to (d);

(f) an institution which is controlled—

    (i) by any person falling within any of sub-paragraphs (a) to (e), or

    (ii) by two or more such persons taken together; or

(g) a body corporate in which—

    (i) any connected person falling within any of sub-paragraphs (a) to (f) has a substantial interest, or

    (ii) two or more such persons, taken together, have a substantial interest.

2.—(1) In paragraph 1(c) "child" includes a stepchild and an illegitimate child.

(2) For the purposes of paragraph 1(e) a person living with another as that person's husband or wife shall be treated as that person's spouse.

3. For the purposes of paragraph 1(f) a person controls an institution if he is able to secure that the affairs of the institution are conducted in accordance with his wishes.

4.—(1) For the purposes of paragraph 1(g) any such connected person as is there mentioned has a substantial interest in a body corporate if the person or institution in question—

(a) is interested in shares comprised in the equity share capital of that body of a nominal value of more than one-fifth of that share capital, or

SCH. 2

(b) is entitled to exercise, or control the exercise of, more than one-fifth of the voting power at any general meeting of that body.

1985 c.6.

(2) The rules set out in Part I of Schedule 13 to the Companies Act 1985 (rules for interpretation of certain provisions of that Act) shall apply for the purposes of sub-paragraph (1) above as they apply for the purposes of section 346(4) of that Act ("connected persons" etc).

(3) In this paragraph "equity share capital" and "share" have the same meaning as in that Act.

Section 47.

SCHEDULE 3

MINOR AND CONSEQUENTIAL AMENDMENTS OF CHARITIES ACT 1960

1. In section 1(2) (constitution etc. of Commissioners), for "servants" substitute "employees".

2. In section 8 (receipt and audit of accounts of charities)—

   (a) omit subsections (1) and (2);

   (b) in subsection (3), for "that the condition and accounts of a charity" substitute ", in the case of a charity which is a company, that the condition and accounts of the charity";

   (c) in subsection (4)(b), for "servant" substitute "employee";

   (d) in subsection (6), omit paragraph (a); and

   (e) omit subsection (7).

3. For section 9 substitute—

"Supply by Commissioners of copies of documents open to public inspection.

9. The Commissioners shall, at the request of any person, furnish him with copies of, or extracts from, any document in their possession which is for the time being open to inspection under this Act."

4. In section 16 (entrusting charity property to official custodian)—

   (a) for subsection (1) substitute—

   "(1) The court may by order—

      (a) vest in the official custodian for charities any land or interest in land held by or in trust for a charity;

      (b) authorise or require the persons in whom any such land or interest is vested to transfer it to him; or

      (c) appoint any person to transfer any such land or interest to him;

   and for this purpose "interest in land" means any interest in land other than such an interest by way of mortgage or other security."; and

   (b) omit subsection (2).

5. In section 17 (supplementary provisions as to property vested in official custodian)—

   (a) in subsection (2)—

      (i) at the beginning insert "Subject to subsection (2A) below,"; and

(ii) for the words from "require him" onwards substitute "execute or do in their own name and on their own behalf if the land or interest were vested in them.";

(b) after that subsection insert—

"(2A) If any land or interest in land is so vested in the official custodian for charities by virtue of an order under section 20 of this Act, the power conferred on the charity trustees by subsection (2) above shall not be exercisable by them in relation to any transaction affecting the land or interest, unless the transaction is authorised by order of the court or of the Commissioners."; and

(c) in each of subsections (4) and (5), after "(2)" insert ", (2A)".

6. In section 18(1)(b) (concurrent jurisdiction with High Court for certain purposes), for "servant" substitute "employee".

7. In section 19(6) (further powers to make schemes or alter application of charitable property)—

(a) omit "or the like reference from the Secretary of State"; and

(b) for "or reference made with a view to a scheme," substitute "for a scheme, or in a case where they act by virtue of subsection (6) or (6A) of that section,".

8. In section 21 (publicity for proceedings under sections 18 and 20 of the Act)—

(a) in subsection (2), after "shall not apply" insert "in the case of an order under section 20(1)(ii), or"; and

(b) in subsection (3), for "servant" substitute "employee".

9. In section 22 (common investment schemes)—

(a) omit subsection (6); and

(b) in subsection (9), omit the words from ", and the" to "endowment" (where last occurring).

10. In section 28 (authorisation by Commissioners of charity proceedings)—

(a) at the end of subsection (3) add "(other than those conferred by section 26A of this Act)."; and

(b) at the end of subsection (6) add ", or to the taking of proceedings by the Commissioners in accordance with section 26A of this Act."

11. In section 30C(1) (charitable companies: status to appear on correspondence, etc.)—

(a) in paragraph (c), omit "by or"; and

(b) in paragraph (e), for "its bills of parcels," substitute "bills rendered by it and in all its".

12. Omit section 31 (protection of expression "common good").

13. In section 32 (general obligation to keep accounts)—

(a) in subsection (2)—

(i) for "seven" substitute "six", and

(ii) for "permit them to be" substitute "consent in writing to their being"; and

(b) for subsection (3) substitute—

"(3) This section applies only to exempt charities."

14. In section 34(2) (manner of executing documents), in paragraph (c), for "and to the persons" onwards substitute "the charity trustees from time to time of the charity and exercisable by such trustees."

15. After section 40 insert—

"Service of orders and directions under this Act.

40A.—(1) This section applies to any order or direction made or given by the Commissioners under this Act.

(2) An order or direction to which this section applies may be served on a person (other than a body corporate)—

(a) by delivering it to that person;

(b) by leaving it at his last known address in the United Kingdom; or

(c) by sending it by post to him at that address.

(3) An order or direction to which this section applies may be served on a body corporate by delivering it or sending it by post—

(a) to the registered or principal office of the body in the United Kingdom, or

(b) if it has no such office in the United Kingdom, to any place in the United Kingdom where it carries on business or conducts its activities (as the case may be).

(4) Any such order or direction may also be served on a person (including a body corporate) by sending it by post to that person at an address notified by that person to the Commissioners for the purposes of this subsection.

(5) In this section any reference to the Commissioners includes, in relation to a direction given under section 6(3) of this Act, a reference to any person conducting an inquiry under that section."

16. In section 41 (enforcement of orders of Commissioners etc.), for paragraph (a) substitute—

"(a) to an order of the Commissioners under section 7(1) of this Act; or".

17. In section 43 (regulations), after subsection (2) insert—

"(2A) Any regulations under this Act may make—

(a) different provision for different cases;

(b) such supplemental, incidental, consequential or transitional provision or savings as the person or persons making them considers or consider appropriate."

18. In section 45 (construction of references to a charity etc.)—

(a) in subsection (3)—

(i) omit "Subject to subsection (9) of section twenty-two of this Act,", and

(ii) for "so expended" substitute "expended for the purposes of
the charity"; and

(b) in subsection (4), for the words from "not having" to "without" substitute "whose income from all sources does not in aggregate amount to more than a specified amount shall be construed—

(i) by reference to the gross revenues of the charity, or

(ii) if the Commissioners so determine, by reference to the amount which they estimate to be the likely amount of those revenues,

but without (in either case)".

19. In section 46 (other definitions)—

(a) in the definition of "permanent endowment" omit ", subject to subsection (9) of section twenty-two of this Act,"; and

(b) at the end add—

"(2) In this Act, except in so far as the context otherwise requires, "document" includes information recorded in any form, and, in relation to information recorded otherwise than in legible form—

(a) any reference to its production shall be construed as a reference to the furnishing of a copy of it in legible form, and

(b) any reference to the furnishing of a copy of, or extract from, it shall accordingly be construed as a reference to the furnishing of a copy of, or extract from, it in legible form.";

and the existing provisions of section 46 (as amended by sub-paragraph (a) above) shall accordingly constitute subsection (1) of that section.

20. In each of sub-paragraphs (1) and (2) of paragraph 2 of Schedule 1 (appointment of assistant commissioners etc.), for "servants" substitute "employees".

21.—(1) Paragraph 3 of Schedule 1 (procedure of Commissioners) shall be amended as follows.

(2) In sub-paragraph (4), for "two shall be the quorum; and" substitute "then—

(a) if not more than four commissioners hold office for the time being, the quorum shall be two commissioners (of whom at least one must be a person having a qualification such as is mentioned in paragraph 1(2) above); and

(b) if five commissioners so hold office, the quorum shall be three commissioners (of whom at least one must be a person having such a qualification);

and".

(3) At the end of the paragraph add—

"(6) It is hereby declared that the power of a commissioner or assistant commissioner to act for and in the name of the Commissioners in accordance with sub-paragraph (3) above may, in particular, be exercised in relation to functions of the Commissioners under sections 6, 20, 20A and 30 of this Act."

22. In Schedule 2 (exempt charities), after paragraph (d) insert—

"(da) the National Gallery Trustees;

(db) the Tate Gallery Trustees;

(dc) the National Portrait Gallery;

(dd) the Wallace Collection Trustees;".

SCHEDULE 4

AMENDMENTS OF CHARITABLE TRUSTEES INCORPORATION ACT 1872

1872 c.24.

1. For section 1 of the Charitable Trustees Incorporation Act 1872 ("the 1872 Act") substitute—

"Incorporation of trustees of a charity.

1.—(1) Where—

    (a) the trustees of a charity, in accordance with section 3 of this Act, apply to the Commissioners for a certificate of incorporation of the trustees as a body corporate, and

    (b) the Commissioners consider that the incorporation of the trustees would be in the interests of the charity,

the Commissioners may grant such a certificate, subject to such conditions or directions as they think fit to insert in it.

(2) The Commissioners shall not, however, grant such a certificate in a case where the charity appears to them to be required to be registered in the register kept by them under section 4 of the Charities Act 1960 but is not so registered.

(3) On the grant of such a certificate—

    (a) the trustees of the charity shall become a body corporate by such name as is specified in the certificate; and

    (b) (without prejudice to the operation of section 5 of this Act) any relevant rights or liabilities of those trustees shall become rights or liabilities of that body.

(4) After their incorporation the trustees—

    (a) may sue and be sued in their corporate name; and

    (b) shall have the same powers, and be subject to the same restrictions and limitations, as respects the holding, acquisition and disposal of property for or in connection with the purposes of the charity as they had or were subject to while unincorporated;

and any relevant legal proceedings that might have been continued or commenced by or against the trustees may be continued or commenced by or against them in their corporate name.

(5) A body incorporated under this section need not have a common seal.

(6) In this section—

    "relevant rights or liabilities" means rights or liabilities in connection with any property vesting in the body in question under section 2 of this Act; and

    "relevant legal proceedings" means legal proceedings in connection with any such property."

2. In section 2 (estate to vest in incorporated body), omit the words from "; and all" onwards.

3. For section 3 of the 1872 Act substitute—

"Applications for incorporation.

3.—(1) Every application to the Commissioners for a certificate of incorporation under this Act shall—

    (a) be in writing and signed by the trustees of the charity concerned; and

    (b) be accompanied by such documents or information as the Commissioners may require for the purpose of the application.

(2) The Commissioners may require—

    (a) any statement contained in any such application, or

    (b) any document or information supplied under subsection (1)(b) above,

to be verified in such manner as they may specify."

4. In section 4 of the 1872 Act (nomination of trustees, etc.), omit the words from "; and the appointment" onwards.

5. In section 5 of the 1872 Act (liability of trustees despite incorporation), omit the words from "; and nothing" onwards.

6. After section 6 of the 1872 Act insert—

"Power of Commissioners to amend certificate of incorporation.

6A.—(1) The Commissioners may amend a certificate of incorporation either on the application of the incorporated body to which it relates or of their own motion.

(2) Before making any such amendment of their own motion, the Commissioners shall by notice in writing—

    (a) inform the trustees of the relevant charity of their proposals, and

    (b) invite those trustees to make representations to them within a time specified in the notice, being not less than one month from the date of the notice.

(3) The Commissioners shall take into consideration any representations made by those trustees within the time so specified, and may then (without further notice) proceed with their proposals either without modification or with such modifications as appear to them to be desirable.

(4) The Commissioners may amend a certificate of incorporation either—

    (a) by making an order specifying the amendment; or

    (b) by issuing a new certificate of incorporation taking account of the amendment."

7. In section 7 of the 1872 Act (Commissioners to keep record of applications for certificates etc. and charge fees for inspection), omit the words from "; and there" onwards.

8. In section 8 of the 1872 Act (enforcement of orders and directions of Commissioners), for the words from "shall also" onwards substitute "section 41 of the Charities Act 1960 (enforcement of orders of Commissioners) shall apply to any trustee who fails to perform or observe any such condition or direction as it applies to a person guilty of disobedience to any such order of the Commissioners as is mentioned in that section."

9. For section 12 of the 1872 Act substitute—

"Execution of documents by incorporated body.

12.—(1) This section has effect as respects the execution of documents by an incorporated body.

(2) If an incorporated body has a common seal, a document may be executed by the body by the affixing of its common seal.

(3) Whether or not it has a common seal, a document may be executed by an incorporated body either—

(a) by being signed by a majority of the trustees of the relevant charity and expressed (in whatever form of words) to be executed by the body; or

(b) by being executed in pursuance of an authority given under subsection (4) below.

(4) For the purposes of subsection (3)(b) above the trustees of the relevant charity in the case of an incorporated body may, subject to the trusts of the charity, confer on any two or more of their number—

(a) a general authority, or

(b) an authority limited in such manner as the trustees think fit,

to execute in the name and on behalf of the body documents for giving effect to transactions to which the body is a party.

(5) An authority under subsection (4) above—

(a) shall suffice for any document if it is given in writing or by resolution of a meeting of the trustees of the relevant charity, notwithstanding the want of any formality that would be required in giving an authority apart from that subsection;

(b) may be given so as to make the powers conferred exercisable by any of the trustees, or may be restricted to named persons or in any other way;

(c) subject to any such restriction, and until it is revoked, shall, notwithstanding any change in the trustees of the relevant charity, have effect as a continuing authority given by the trustees from time to time of the charity and exercisable by such trustees.

(6) In any authority under subsection (4) above to execute a document in the name and on behalf of an incorporated body there shall, unless the contrary intention appears, be implied authority also to execute it for the body in the name and on behalf of the official custodian for charities or of any other person, in any case in which the trustees could do so.

(7) A document duly executed by an incorporated body which makes it clear on its face that it is intended by the person or persons making it to be a deed has effect, upon delivery, as a deed; and it shall be presumed, unless a contrary intention is proved, to be delivered upon its being so executed.

(8) In favour of a purchaser a document shall be deemed to have been duly executed by such a body if it purports to be signed—

(a) by a majority of the trustees of the relevant charity, or

(b) by such of the trustees of the relevant charity as are authorised by the trustees of that charity to execute it in the name and on behalf of the body,

and, where the document makes it clear on its face that it is intended by the person or persons making it to be a deed, it shall be deemed to have been delivered upon its being executed.

For this purpose "purchaser" means a purchaser in good faith for valuable consideration and includes a lessee, mortgagee or other person who for valuable consideration acquires an interest in property.

Power of Commissioners to dissolve incorporated body.

12A.—(1) Where the Commissioners are satisfied—

(a) that an incorporated body has no assets or does not operate, or

(b) that the relevant charity in the case of an incorporated body has ceased to exist, or

(c) that the institution previously constituting, or treated by them as constituting, any such charity has ceased to be, or (as the case may be) was not at the time of the body's incorporation, a charity, or

(d) that the purposes of the relevant charity in the case of an incorporated body have been achieved so far as is possible or are in practice incapable of being achieved,

they may of their own motion make an order dissolving the body as from such date as is specified in the order.

(2) Where the Commissioners are satisfied, on the application of the trustees of the relevant charity in the case of an incorporated body, that it would be in the interests of the charity for that body to be dissolved, the Commissioners may make an order dissolving the body as from such date as is specified in the order.

(3) Subject to subsection (4) below, an order made under this section with respect to an incorporated body shall have the effect of vesting in the trustees of the relevant charity, in trust for that charity, all property for the time being vested—

(a) in the body, or

(b) in any other person (apart from the official custodian for charities),

in trust for that charity.

(4) If the Commissioners so direct in the order—

(a) all or any specified part of that property shall, instead of vesting in the trustees of the relevant charity, vest—

(i) in a specified person as trustee for, or nominee of, that charity, or

(ii) in such persons (other than the trustees of the relevant charity) as may be specified;

(b) any specified investments, or any specified class or description of investments, held by any person in trust for the relevant charity shall be transferred—

(i) to the trustees of that charity, or

(ii) to any such person or persons as is or are mentioned in paragraph (a)(i) or (ii) above;

and for this purpose "specified" means specified by the Commissioners in the order.

(5) Where an order to which this subsection applies is made with respect to an incorporated body—

(a) any rights or liabilities of the body shall become rights or liabilities of the trustees of the relevant charity; and

(b) any legal proceedings that might have been continued or commenced by or against the body may be continued or commenced by or against those trustees.

(6) Subsection (5) above applies to any order under this section by virtue of which—

(a) any property vested as mentioned in subsection (3) above is vested—

(i) in the trustees of the relevant charity, or

(ii) in any person as trustee for, or nominee of, that charity; or

(b) any investments held by any person in trust for the relevant charity are required to be transferred—

(i) to the trustees of that charity, or

(ii) to any person as trustee for, or nominee of, that charity.

(7) Any order made by the Commissioners under this section may be varied or revoked by a further order so made."

10. For section 14 of the 1872 Act substitute—

"Interpretation.   14. In this Act—

"charity" has the same meaning as in the Charities Act 1960;

"the Commissioners" means the Charity Commissioners;

"incorporated body" means a body incorporated under section 1 of this Act;

"the relevant charity", in relation to an incorporated body, means the charity the trustees of which have been incorporated as that body;

"the trustees", in relation to a charity, means the charity trustees within the meaning of the Charities Act 1960."

11. Omit the Schedule (particulars to be supplied for the purposes of section 3 of the Act).

SCHEDULE 5

AMENDMENTS OF REDUNDANT CHURCHES AND OTHER RELIGIOUS BUILDINGS ACT 1969

1. For section 4 of the Redundant Churches and Other Religious Buildings Act 1969 ("the 1969 Act") substitute— 1969 c.22.

"Transfer of certain redundant places of public worship.

4.—(1) Subject to subsections (9) and (10) below, this section applies to any premises if—

    (a) the premises are held by or in trust for a charity ("the relevant charity"), and

    (b) the whole or part of the premises has been used as a place of public worship; but

    (c) the premises are not a church subject to the provisions of the Pastoral Measure 1983.

(2) If the court is satisfied, with respect to any premises to which this section applies ("the relevant premises")—

    (a) that those premises are no longer required (whether wholly or in part) for use as a place of public worship, and

    (b) that one of the following, namely—

        (i) the Secretary of State,

        (ii) the Commission, or

        (iii) a prescribed charity,

    is or are willing to enter into an agreement to acquire those premises by way of gift or for a consideration other than full consideration, but

    (c) that it is not within the powers of the persons in whom those premises are vested to carry out such an agreement except by virtue of this section,

the court may, under its jurisdiction with respect to charities, establish a scheme for the making and carrying out of such an agreement.

(3) A scheme established under subsection (2) above may, if it appears to the court proper to do so, provide for the acquirer of the relevant premises also to acquire (whether by gift or for a consideration other than full consideration or otherwise)—

    (a) any land held by or in trust for the relevant charity which is contiguous or adjacent to those premises; and

    (b) any objects which are or have been ordinarily kept on those premises.

(4) In subsections (2) and (3) above, in relation to the acquisition of the relevant premises or the acquisition of any land or object—

    (a) references to acquisition by the Secretary of State are references to acquisition by him under section 5 of the Historic Buildings and Ancient Monuments Act 1953 (acquisition by him of buildings of historic or architectural interest); and

    (b) references to acquisition by the Commission are references to acquisition by them under section 5A of that Act (acquisition by them of buildings of historic or architectural interest).

(5) A scheme established under subsection (2) above may also provide for conferring on the acquirer of the relevant premises—

    (a) such rights of way over any land held by or in trust for the relevant charity as appear to the court to be necessary—

        (i) for the purpose of the discharge of the acquirer's functions in relation to those premises or to any land acquired under the scheme, or

        (ii) for giving to the public reasonable access to those premises or to any such land, and

    (b) so far as is necessary for the purpose of the discharge of such functions or the giving of such access, any rights of way enjoyed by persons attending services at those premises.

(6) The Charity Commissioners may, on the application of the acquirer of the relevant premises, by order establish a scheme under section 18 of the Charities Act 1960 (Commissioners' concurrent jurisdiction with the High Court for certain purposes) making provision for the restoration of the relevant premises, or part of them, to use as a place of public worship.

(7) The Charity Commissioners may so establish any such scheme notwithstanding—

    (a) anything in subsection (4) of section 18 of that Act, or

    (b) that the relevant charity has ceased to exist;

and if the relevant charity has ceased to exist, any such scheme may provide for the constitution of a charity by or in trust for which the relevant premises are to be held on the restoration of those premises, or part of them, to use as a place of public worship.

(8) The Charity Commissioners shall have the same jurisdiction and powers in relation to the establishment of a scheme under subsection (2) above as they have under the provisions of section 18 of the Charities Act 1960 (except subsection (6)) in relation to the establishment of a scheme for the administration of a charity; and section 21 of that Act (publicity for proceedings under section 18, etc.) shall accordingly have effect in relation to the establishment of a scheme under subsection (2) above as it has effect in relation to the establishment of a scheme for the administration of a charity.

(9) In relation to the Commission—

    (a) this section only applies to any premises falling within subsection (1) above if they are situated in England, and

    (b) references in this section to land are references only to land situated in England.

(10) In relation to a prescribed charity, this section only applies to any premises falling within subsection (1) above if they constitute either—

    (a) a listed building within the meaning of the Planning (Listed Buildings and Conservation Areas) Act 1990, or

(b) a scheduled monument within the meaning of the Ancient Monuments and Archaeological Areas Act 1979.

Sch. 5

(11) The Secretary of State may direct that any charity specified in the direction shall be a prescribed charity for the purposes of this section; and any direction under this subsection may be varied or revoked by a further direction given by the Secretary of State.

(12) References in this section to the acquirer of the relevant premises are references to the person or body acquiring those premises by virtue of a scheme established under subsection (2) above.

(13) In this section and section 5 below—

"the Commission" means the Historic Buildings and Monuments Commission for England;

"premises" includes a part of a building;

"prescribed charity" shall be construed by reference to subsection (11) above;

and sections 45 and 46 of the Charities Act 1960 (interpretation) shall have effect for the purposes of this section and section 5 below as they have effect for the purposes of that Act."

2. For section 5 of the 1969 Act substitute—

"Trusts for repair etc. of premises to continue after transfer under section 4.

5.—(1) Where any premises to which section 4 of this Act applies are acquired by the Secretary of State, the Commission or a prescribed charity in pursuance of that section, any property of a charity whose purposes include—

(a) the repair and maintenance of those premises, or

(b) the provision of objects for keeping on those premises, or

(c) the maintenance of objects ordinarily kept there,

shall (subject to subsection (2) below) continue to be applicable for that purpose so long as the premises remain vested in the Secretary of State, the Commission or the prescribed charity, as the case may be.

(2) If so provided by the scheme under which the agreement for the acquisition of any such premises is made, subsection (1) above shall have effect in relation to the premises subject to and in accordance with any specified provisions of the scheme.

(3) Subsection (13) of section 4 of this Act has effect for the purposes of this section."

SCHEDULE 6

MINOR AND CONSEQUENTIAL AMENDMENTS

CLERGY PENSIONS MEASURE 1961 (No.3)

1. In section 33 (preservation of restrictions on certain transactions)—

    (a) for "section twenty-nine of the Charities Act 1960" substitute "section 32 of the Charities Act 1992"; and

    (b) for "said Act" substitute "Charities Act 1960".

FINANCE ACT 1963 (C.25)

2. In section 65(2)(a) (miscellaneous exemptions), after "1960" insert "or any common deposit scheme under section 22A of that Act".

CATHEDRALS MEASURE 1963 (No.2)

3. In section 20(2)(iii) (consents to disposal of land by cathedral bodies), for "section twenty-nine of the Charities Act 1960" substitute "section 32 of the Charities Act 1992".

LEASEHOLD REFORM ACT 1967 (C.88)

4. In section 23(4) (grant of new tenancy), for "section 29 of the Charities Act 1960" substitute "section 32 of the Charities Act 1992".

SHARING OF CHURCH BUILDINGS ACT 1969 (C.38)

5. In section 8(3) (shared buildings), for the words from the beginning to "Commissioners)" substitute "Section 32 of the Charities Act 1992 (restrictions on dispositions of charity land)".

LOCAL GOVERNMENT ACT 1972 (C.70)

6. In section 131(3) (savings)—

    (a) for the words from "section 29" to "property)" substitute "section 32 of the Charities Act 1992 (restrictions on disposition of charity land)"; and

    (b) for "subsection (3)(a) of that section" substitute "section 32(9)(a) of that Act".

FIRE PRECAUTIONS (LOANS) ACT 1973 (C.11)

7. In section 1(7) (loans to meet certain expenditure), for the words from the beginning to "property)" substitute "Section 34 of the Charities Act 1992 (which restricts the charging of charity property)".

THEATRES TRUST ACT 1976 (C.27)

8. In section 2(2)(d) (powers of trustees), for "section 29 of the Charities Act 1960" substitute "sections 32 and 34 of the Charities Act 1992".

LOCAL GOVERNMENT (MISCELLANEOUS PROVISIONS) ACT 1982 (C.30)

9. In Schedule 4 (street trading), for paragraph 1(2)(j) substitute—

    "(j) the doing of anything authorised by any permit or order under Part III of the Charities Act 1992."

CIVIC GOVERNMENT (SCOTLAND) ACT 1982 (C. 45)

10. In section 119(6)(d) (grounds for refusal of permission for public charitable collection in Scotland)—

    (a) after "under", where secondly occurring, insert "this section or"; and

    (b) after "section", where secondly occurring, insert "or under Part III of the Charities Act 1992 or regulations made under section 73 of that Act".

COMPANIES ACT 1985 (C.6)

11. In each of the following provisions, namely—

    (a) section 209(1)(c) (interests to be disregarded for purposes of general disclosure provisions), and

    (b) paragraph 11(b) of Schedule 13 (interests to be disregarded for purposes of provisions relating to disclosure by directors etc.),

after "section 22" insert "or 22A".

HOUSING ACT 1985 (C.68)

12. For paragraph 12 of Schedule 1 substitute—

    "12. A licence to occupy a dwelling-house is not a secure tenancy if—

    (a) the dwelling-house is an almshouse, and

    (b) the licence was granted by or on behalf of a charity which—

        (i) is authorised under its trusts to maintain the dwelling-house as an almshouse, and

        (ii) has no power under its trusts to grant a tenancy of the dwelling-house;

and in this paragraph "almshouse" means any premises maintained as an almshouse, whether they are called an almshouse or not; and "trusts", in relation to a charity, means the provisions establishing it as a charity and regulating its purposes and administration, whether those provisions take effect by way of trust or not."

HOUSING ASSOCIATIONS ACT 1985 (C.69)

13.—(1) In section 10(1) (excepted dispositions), for "section 29 of the Charities Act 1960" substitute "sections 32 and 34 of the Charities Act 1992".

(2) In section 26(2) (accounting requirements), for the words from "section 8" onwards substitute "sections 19 to 23 of the Charities Act 1992 (charity accounts)."

(3) In section 35(2)(c) (power to transfer housing to local housing authority), for the words from "section" to "Commissioners)" substitute "section 32 of the Charities Act 1992 (restrictions on dispositions of charity land)".

FINANCIAL SERVICES ACT 1986 (C.60)

14. In section 45(1)(j) (miscellaneous exemptions), after "section 22" insert "or 22A".

COAL INDUSTRY ACT 1987 (C.3)

15. In section 5 (power of Commissioners to make schemes relating to coal industry trusts), for subsection (8) substitute—

SCH. 6

"(8) Sections 18(3), (8), (10) to (12), 19(1) to (5) and (7) and 21 of the Charities Act 1960 shall apply in relation to the powers of the Charity Commissioners and the making of schemes under this section as they apply in relation to their powers and the making of schemes under that Act; and sections 40(1) to (4), 40A and 42 of that Act shall apply to orders and decisions under this section as they apply to orders and decisions under that Act.

(8A) The Commissioners shall not proceed under section 19 of that Act (as applied by subsection (8) above) without the like application, and the like notice to the trustees of the trust in question, as would be required if they were proceeding under subsection (1) above; but on any application made with a view to a scheme under subsection (1) above the Commissioners may proceed under that subsection or under section 19 of that Act (as so applied) as appears to them appropriate."

REVERTER OF SITES ACT 1987 (C.15)

16. In section 4(4) (supplementary provisions), after "sections 40" insert ", 40A".

INCOME AND CORPORATION TAXES ACT 1988 (C.1)

17. After paragraph 3 of Schedule 20 (charities: qualifying investments and loans) insert—

"3A. Any investment in a common deposit fund established under section 22A of the Charities Act 1960 or in any similar fund established for the exclusive benefit of charities by or under any enactment relating to any particular charities or class of charities."

Section 78(2).

SCHEDULE 7

REPEALS

Chapter	Short title	Extent of repeal
1872 c.24.	Charitable Trustees Incorporation Act 1872.	In section 2, the words from "; and all" onwards. In section 4, the words from "; and the appointment" onwards. In section 5, the words from "; and nothing" onwards. In section 7, the words from "; and there" onwards. The Schedule.
1916 c.31.	Police, Factories, &c. (Miscellaneous Provisions) Act 1916.	The whole Act.
1939 c.44.	House to House Collections Act 1939.	The whole Act.
1940 c.31.	War Charities Act 1940.	The whole Act.
1948 c.29.	National Assistance Act 1948.	Section 41.
1958 c.49.	Trading Representations (Disabled Persons) Act 1958.	Section 1(2)(b).

Chapter	Short title	Extent of repeal
1959 c.72.	Mental Health Act 1959.	Section 8(3).
1960 c.58.	Charities Act 1960.	In section 4(6), the words from "and any person" onwards. Section 6(6) and (9). Section 7(4). Section 8(1), (2), (6)(a) and (7). Section 16(2). In section 19(6), the words "or the like reference from the Secretary of State". In section 22, subsection (6) and, in subsection (9), the words from ", and the" to "endowment" (where last occurring). Section 27. Section 29. In section 30C(1)(c), the words "by or". Section 31. Section 44. In section 45(3), the words "Subject to subsection (9) of section twenty-two of this Act,". In section 46, the words ", subject to subsection (9) of section twenty-two of this Act,". In Schedule 1, in paragraph 1(3), the words "Subject to sub-paragraph (6) below,". In Schedule 6, the entry relating to the War Charities Act 1940.
1966 c.42.	Local Government Act 1966.	In Schedule 3, in column 1 of Part II, paragraph 20.
1968 c.60.	Theft Act 1968.	In Schedule 2, in Part III, the entry relating to the House to House Collections Act 1939.
1970 c.42.	Local Authority Social Services Act 1970.	In Schedule 1, the entry relating to section 41 of the National Assistance Act 1948.
1972 c.70.	Local Government Act 1972.	Section 210(8). In Schedule 29, paragraphs 22 and 23.
1983 c.41.	Health and Social Services and Social Security Adjudications Act 1983.	Section 30(3).
1983 c.47.	National Heritage Act 1983.	In Schedule 4, paragraphs 13 and 14.

Chapter	Short title	Extent of repeal
1985 c.9.	Companies Consolidation (Consequential Provisions) Act 1985.	In Schedule 2, the entry relating to section 30(1) of the Charities Act 1960.
1985 c.20.	Charities Act 1985.	The whole Act.
1986 c.41.	Finance Act 1986.	Section 33.

PRINTED IN THE UNITED KINGDOM BY PAUL FREEMAN
Controller and Chief Executive of Her Majesty's Stationery Office
and Queen's Printer of Acts of Parliament